Augsburg College
George Sverdrup Library
Minneapolis, Minnesota 55404

VILLAGE GOVERNMENT IN INDIA

Village Government in India

A Case Study

by
RALPH H. RETZLAFF

ASIA PUBLISHING HOUSE
BOMBAY/CALCUTTA/NEW DELHI/MADRAS
LONDON/NEW YORK

© RALPH H. RETZLAFF
1962

PRINTED IN INDIA

BY J.M. D'SOUZA AT THE NATIONAL PRINTING WORKS,
10 DARYAGANJ, DELHI AND PUBLISHED BY P. S.
JAYASINGHE, ASIA PUBLISHING HOUSE, BOMBAY

To
the villagers of Khalapur, whose patience, goodwill and understanding have made this study possible.

Acknowledgements

THE author cannot fully acknowledge the debt which he owes to the members of the Cornell University Field Research Project, with whom he was associated and who preceded him in conducting research in the village of Khalapur. Dr M. E. Opler, Director of the Cornell University India Program, initially suggested the research program from which this study resulted, and made possible the field research involved through a subsidiary grant from that originally awarded to the Program by the Ford Foundation. The author is particularly indebted to Sachchidanand Awasty, whose help and cooperation was invaluable in gathering the data upon which the study is based. The other members of the Project, Usha Baghat, John J. Gumperz, John T. Hitchcock, Gurdeep Jaispal, Rajendra K. Jaiswal, Edward E. LeClair, J. Michael Mahar, Pauline M. Mahar, Vishwa Mohan, Jack Planalp, R. Prakash Rao, Deo Dutt Sharma, Shyam Narian Singh, Subaghya Taneja, A. Vaidyanathan, Dara Vania, and Toshio Yatsushiro are perhaps the only ones who can fully appreciate the extent of cooperation and advice given the author in this inter-disciplinary field research project.

Discussions with Dr M. N. Srinivas, of Delhi University, and Dr V. Nath, formerly Director of the Program Evaluation Organization, Planning Commission, Government of India, were most valuable in helping the author formulate aspects of the problem.

I am particularly indebted to my wife, Kathryn, whose patience, encouragement and willingness to retype innumerable drafts were important factors in seeing this manuscript through to completion.

The responsibility for the facts presented and the conclusions drawn is solely that of the author.

Contents

	Introduction	1
I.	Traditional Village Organization	13
II.	The Period of British Rule	27
III.	The Introduction of Panchayat Raj	49
IV.	The Functioning of the First Gaon Panchayat	62
V.	Election of the Second Gaon Panchayat	90
VI.	Conclusion	114

Appendix A: Functions of Gaon Panchayats	127
Appendix B: Tax Schedule	130
Glossary of Terms and Names	133
Index	137

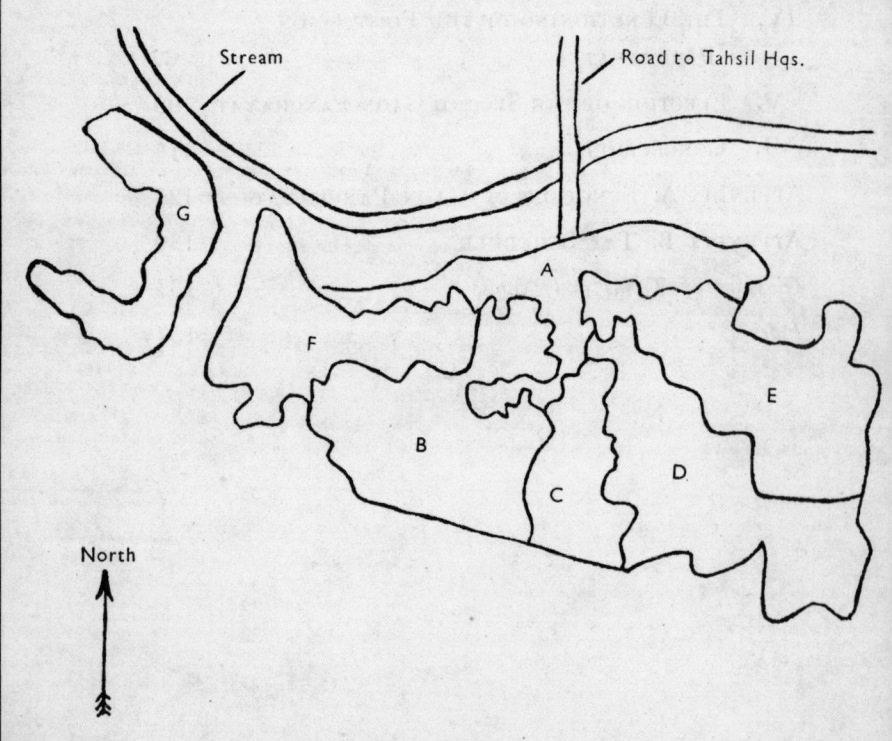

Introduction

THE Indian village is today the focus of considerable activity generated by Centre and State Government authorities, as well as by a number of voluntary organizations. A common feature of all these activities is the intent to bring about a change in rural living standards and conditions. Some have as their stated purpose the introduction of new techniques, information and ideas. Others are aimed at bringing about alterations in the pattern of property relationships and land tenure. Still others aim at the creation of differing types of institutions within the village which may serve as vehicles for the implementation of the aforementioned activities, as well as innumerable other programmes. The two basic types of institutions which government has sought to create in rural India are cooperatives and panchayats, and of the two, the most extensive activity has been connected with panchayats.

Considerable controversy has surrounded the institution called the village panchayat, particularly with respect to its ancient origins, and the effects of British rule on it. In the pre-Independence period the Indian National Congress was strongly committed to the passage of legislation for the purpose of creating self-governing institutions at the village level, or strengthening such institutions where they still existed. This commitment stemmed in part from the influence of Gandhi, who strongly supported proposals for decentralization of political power and put an emphasis on the self-sufficiency of the village in all respects. It also stemmed from the commitment of the nationalists to the creation of a democratic political system which they inferred involved creating institutions of self-government at all levels of the Indian polity.

To question the wisdom, or effectiveness, of introducing institutions of self-government based upon certain assumptions about the social and economic order, which were in fact not operative in rural India, was to commit heresy in the nationalist view. This was seen as supporting the British contention that Indians were not fit to govern themselves. That these two were totally different propositions was never acknowledged or even enquired into, and thus no attempt was made to delineate those changes which would be required in the existing social and economic order, and the means that would have to be employed to achieve them, if institutions of democratic local self-government were to operate effectively in the rural Indian setting.

In the immediate post-Independence period one of the first steps taken by many of the State Governments was to pass legislation, or in some cases amend existing legislation passed during the British period, on the basis of which panchayats were to be created in the villages of India. The legislation passed in the State of Uttar Pradesh, the State in which the present case study was carried out, was considered by the Centre Government and most of the States as something of a model. By the year 1953, the States in India were covered by panchayat legislation, having either adopted new acts, or modified existing ones.

The "legislative phase" was followed by an "administrative phase," in which areas of jurisdiction were demarcated, elections held, and village panchayats brought into being. Administrative organizations were set up to supervise these new bodies, and the inevitable plethora of rules and forms for these purposes soon came into being.

At this point most of the State Governments relaxed, feeling that they had fully discharged a long-standing obligation, and confident that these new panchayats would make useful contributions in raising rural living standards and conditions. With the exception of one or two States, such as the former Saurashtra State, the distribution of the portfolio of local self-government in the State Cabinets was at a low level of priority, and was rarely assumed by the Chief Minister or one of the more powerful members in the Cabinet.

A closer look at what has been accomplished since the implementation of the legislation reveals several serious shortcomings in the various panchayat programmes. Many of them are evident in the accompanying case study, and it may be of some use to note them briefly here. First, one uniform characteristic of these panchayat acts, of which Uttar Pradesh Panchayat Raj Act was typical, was the complete absence of any realistic assessment of the existing situation in the villages. The framers of the Act, and the authorities charged with its implementation both had failed to consider the problems posed by the prior existence of informal decision-making bodies, which had been functioning in some instances for centuries in a great number of villages. These informal bodies were familiar to the villagers. They were based on local customs and usages, and over time had proven their utility and effectiveness.

In failing to evaluate the existence and importance of these bodies, it also went largely unnoticed that they were controlled by individuals and groups generally opposed to radical social, economic and political change, and who could therefore be expected either to resist any attempt to introduce new institutions which aimed at such types of change, or to attempt to gain control of them and thus be in a position to insure that the existing order was not upset.

The legislation also overlooked the realities of the rural pattern of social, economic and political organization, which was characteristically hierarchical and paternalistic. The premises underlying the introduction of adult suffrage, namely, that each resident of the village would exercise a free choice in the selection of members of the village executive council, did not accord with reality, particularly when to this was added the further condition that village elections were to be held by an open show of hands. Marked disparity in economic and social status had traditionally concentrated political power in the hands of a relatively small rural elite. The manner in which these new institutions were brought into being did little, at the outset, to alter the power position of that rural elite. This virtually negated the possibility of the panchayats becoming the agents of radical social and economic change, or of serving as the vehicles for the rapid introduction of democratic principles and procedures into rural life. The basic commitment of the elites in rural India was toward the maintenance of the existing forms of organization. Where less privileged social groups begin to openly support change, it was exceedingly difficult for them to wrest control of these new institutions from the tradition-oriented elite. This was true even when caste and community did not stand as barriers to those who sought change and a closer approximation of the democratic process.

A somewhat different, but equally important, consideration was that the legislation setting up the new panchayats was complex, lengthy and detailed. It was certainly not drafted with the preciseness and simplicity that would have made its provisions readily understandable to a rural population over 85 per cent illiterate and unsophisticated in the ways of legislative interpretation. The Act charged the villagers with a broad (one is tempted to say all-encompassing) range of duties and responsibilities. The procedures and forms framed under the Act reflected the biases of those who had been drawn from the traditional administrative departments to staff the rapidly expanded Panchayat Raj Department. In particular, it reflected the "Revenue Department approach," characteristically concerned with reducing matters to a statistical form and imbued with a regulatory, static approach to rural Indian society.

During the period under review in the accompanying study, villages throughout India felt the impact not only of the panchayat programmes, but in many instances of the multi-faceted land reform programmes, as well as the Community Project and National Extension Service programmes. In Uttar Pradesh, as in many other States, the newly created panchayats were brought into these activities and utilized in various ways to help achieve the ends of the land reform and rural development programmes.

The Planning Commission strongly supported this approach, and argued that village panchayats were the institutions through which social and economic changes would be effectively introduced in the rural areas. The support given these institutions by the Planning Commission, however, was based upon a much more realistic assessment of the changes required in the rural scene if the panchayats were to be effective instruments of democratic local self-government. A good example of this approach is to be found in a paper prepared by Tarlok Singh, Additional Secretary, Planning Commission.[1] In it he argues that the attempt to place the village panchayat at the centre of village development is, in fact, an effort to establish a new institution under an old name. In order to get adequate results from established village panchayats it is necessary to view the institution as a part of a larger process, namely, the fundamental reconstruction of the social and economic relations within rural society. This move, he contends, will succeed in the measure which:

(1) the village panchayat can function within a more or less homogeneous social structure in which different sections of the community are moved by common loyalties and urges, and
(2) the economic basis of village life is expanded and strengthened.

Relative equality of status, he contends, is a fundamental requisite of a homogeneous social structure, as is also the absence of large disparities in the ownership of land, the primary source of employment and wealth in rural India.

If any single common thread can be found in the numerous research studies carried out by Indian and Western anthropologists and sociologists in rural India since Independence, it is that the conditions (or should I say pre-conditions?) cited above by Tarlok Singh are not presently operative in Indian villages. This point is made in a very interesting essay by Daniel

[1] "The Village Panchayat and the Pattern of Village Development," July 1954-October 1955, mimeo.

Thorner,[2] in which he reviews the findings of many of these village studies and comes to the general conclusion that "... to approach the goal of rural economic development through the agency of the existing village panchayats only would appear to be an exercise in frustration."[3]

One of the principal features supporting the hierarchically organized rural society has been the concentration of land ownership. In most Indian villages the bulk of the village lands are held by the members of one or two caste groups, and this has served to give them a virtual stranglehold on the village economy. The land reform measures adopted in the post-Independence period were aimed at altering this situation and reducing the disparities in this respect. But the studies of Thorner,[4] Dandekar and Khudanpur,[5] and Khusro,[6] as well as the Reports of the Committees of the Panel on Land Reforms,[7] appointed by the Planning Commission, all support the view that regardless of whatever else they may have achieved, the land reform programmes have not had the desired

---

[2] "The Village Panchayat as a Vehicle of Change," *The Indian Yearbook of International Affairs*, 1953 (ed.) Charles Henry Alexandrowicz (Madras: University of Madras Press, 1953), pp. 75-85.

[3] *Ibid.*, p. 85.

[4] Daniel Thorner, *The Agrarian Prospect in India* (Delhi: University of Delhi Press, 1956).

[5] V.M. Dandekar and G.J. Khudanpur, *Working of Bombay Tenancy Act 1958, Report of Investigation* (Poona: Gokhale Institute of Politics and Economics, 1957).

[6] A.M. Khusro, *Economic and Social Effects of Jagirdari Abolition and Land Reforms in Hyderabad* (Hyderabad: Osmania University Press, 1958).

[7] Government of India, Planning Commission, *Reports of the Committee of the Panel on Land Reforms* (Delhi: Manager of Publications, Government of India, 1959).

effect of reducing the wide economic disparities that characterize the average Indian village. The more recent attempts to introduce joint cooperative farming and to set ceilings on agricultural holdings are, in a sense, tacit admissions that these conditions relating to land holdings still persist in rural India.

With the passage of time it became increasingly evident that few village panchayats were fulfilling the functions with which they were charged, and that many were either inoperative or functioning in a manner contrary to the basic democratic character of the legislation under which they had been created. This point was incontrovertably made in what was at that time the only study of village panchayats made by a government organization, based on actual field observations of their operation; a study made by the Programme Evaluation Organization of the Planning Commission.[8] This appraisal was also voiced by the team appointed to study Community Projects and the National Extension Service.[9] Their report (referred to hereafter as the Mehta Committee Report) opened what might be termed a new phase in the development of local self-government in India. The recommendations of the Mehta Committee, which were later approved by the National Development Council, called for the creation of a three tiered structure of local self-governing bodies throughout rural India. It was

[8] Government of India, Planning Commission, Programme Evaluation Organization, *A Study of Panchayats* (Delhi: Manager of Publications, Government of India, 1958). The Study was carried out in 1956-57 and was originally published as Chapter IV of the P.E.O.'s *Fifth Evaluation Report*.

[9] Government of India, Planning Commission, Committee on Plan Projects, *Report of the Team for the Study of Community Projects and National Extension Service*, 3 Vols. (New Delhi: Committee on Plan Projects, 1957-58).

proposed that the existing village panchayats form the base of this structure, and that local self-governing bodies be created at the Community Development Block and District levels. It was further suggested that virtually all programmes of economic development which would eventually affect the rural areas, be channelled through this structure. Already, in half a dozen States, led by Rajasthan and Andhra Pradesh, legislation has been passed to bring into being this pattern of rural government organization, and the system has been in operation in the two aforementioned States since Fall 1959.

To a certain extent consideration has been given to the problem of adapting village panchayats to this new system, called Panchayati Raj. Thus, in every State which has adopted this approach, amendments have been made in the existing panchayat acts. But in almost every case (here Rajasthan is an exception), the alteration of these acts has been confined to minor amendments, and few attempts have been made to face squarely the implications of the issues raised by both Tarlok Singh and Daniel Thorner.

Apart from the study of the Programme Evaluation Organization in 1956-57, mentioned above (and a later, similar study in 1959-60), no other field studies have been made which specifically attempt to ascertain how village panchayats actually operate, and to what extent disparities of social and economic status pose barriers, insuperable or otherwise, to the effective participation of all strata of village society in these self-governing institutions.

As an increasing number of States adopt the system of Panchayati Raj it is imperative that a thorough and critical evaluation be made of the existing operation of village panchayats. This becomes particularly urgent since the Panchayati Raj system is based in part on indirect election, with membership of the two higher bodies being composed, primarily, of representatives initially selected to serve on the village panchayat. My own observation is that in certain States these bodies are largely, and in some areas entirely, dominated by the landed elements in rural society, and that the provisions for co-option of unrepresented elements included in most acts have done little to mitigate this strong social bias.

The case study which follows indicates, however, that the situation is not as grim or barren of hope as some critics, such as Thorner, might make it out to be. Studies by sociologists and anthropologists (as well as the author's own personal observations) bear witness to the fact that the existence of what is loosely termed factionalism within a dominant caste in a village has led to the necessity of one or the other faction seeking the support of lower caste elements in such things as village panchayat elections. As a price for this support, some change, however modest, is made in the position of these lower caste groups, both in terms of tangible economic rewards, as well as in less tangible alterations in status relationships. The effects stemming from the opportunity of lower caste members to secure education and acquire positions in the government services is less perceptible in the brief time span that has elapsed, but this is also an important factor making for change in rural India.

Another effect of the introduction of Panchayati Raj has been that political parties have felt obliged to move to capture control of these bodies. (Heretofore most parties had agreed to abstain from contesting elections on a party basis at levels lower than the District.) The emergence of educated leaders from the lower caste groups, able to command substantial blocs of votes, has already begun to force political leaders to become more responsive to the wishes of these groups, and will make it increasingly difficult for the dominant rural elite to retain its control over, and relatively exclusive access to, the benefits of social and economic development that have been flowing into the rural areas during the past decade. These are not changes which take place overnight. They reproduce in many respects the pattern accompanying the extension of democracy in the West, a pattern which took several centuries. It will certainly take much less time in India, and one important factor which can contribute to speeding up such a process will be a realistic assessment by State Governments of the working of local self-government in the rural areas, and the steps necessary to remove the impediments to broadening access to political power and the benefits of economic development. The interests of political self-preservation would seem to dictate this. If this is not done by the existing parties in power at the State level, others, far less reluctant, will sooner or later seize the opportunity to do so.

I
Traditional Village Organization

NINETY miles north of Delhi, in Saharanpur District in Western Uttar Pradesh, lies the village of Khalapur. The only significant difference between it and the villages of the surrounding area is that Khalapur's population of over 5,000 is about three to four times that of the other villages. Its narrow lanes and squat mud huts surrounded by fields of sugar cane, wheat and pulse are characteristic of this part of North India.

Four miles to the west of Khalapur is the Grand Trunk road, which begins in Delhi and goes on to Saharanpur. A recently built all-weather road connects the village to the Tahsil Headquarters, six miles to the Northeast. The Tahsil Headquarters, Deoband, is a main stop on the Northern Railway running from Delhi to Ambala. There are two sugar cane processing mills in the area and Khalapur is located midway between them. One mill is on the outskirts of the Tahsil Headquarters, and the other lies six miles to the south of Khalapur. The farmlands on the Western side of the village are serviced by a branch of the Ganges Canal. It was the introduction of the branch canal, about thirty years ago, which changed the agricultural cash crop pattern of the area from wheat and pulse to sugar cane.

There are members of 36 castes residing in Khalapur. Of these, ten comprise 82 per cent of the population. They are: rajpūt, landowning agriculturists (42 per cent); chamār, landless agricultural labourers (12 per cent); brahman, priestly caste, though some are landowners (5.5 per cent); bhangī, sweepers (4.1 per cent); garariya, goat herders (3.8 per cent); bạrhai, carpenters (3.6 per cent); kahār, water carriers (3 per cent); banyā, merchants (3 per cent); teli, oil pressers (2.8 per cent); and jatiya chamār, cobblers (1.9 per cent).

The rajpūts are what is generally referred to by social scientists as the "dominant caste"[1] in the village. Ninety per cent of the total land area owned by the villagers, 6,023 acres, is owned by members of the rajpūt caste. The principal source of income in the village is agriculture. Those castes not engaged in agriculture as a primary occupation, either as cultivator-owners, tenants, or landless labourers, are nevertheless tied to the agricultural economy by virtue of their traditional service relationships with the dominant land-owning caste. This pattern of traditional service relationships, involving castes such as the blacksmiths, carpenters, potters, washermen, barbers, etc., is generally called the jajman-parjan system,[2] and in Khalapur is

---

[1] M.N. Srinivas, "The Dominant Caste in Rampura," *American Anthropologist*, Vol. 61, No. 1 (February 1959), pp. 1-16.

[2] For a discussion of the jajman-parjan system, or jajmani system as it is often referred to, see: William H. Wiser, *The Hindu Jajmani System*, Lucknow: Lucknow Publishing House 1936; Thomas O. Biedelman, *A Comparative Analysis of the Jajmani System*, Locust Valley, New York: J. J. Augustin, 1959; Harold A. Gould, "The Hindu Jajmani System: A Case Study of Economic Particularism," *Southwestern Journal of Anthropology*, Vol. 14, No. 4 (Winter 1958), pp. 428-37; Edward B. Harper, "Two Systems of Economic Exchange in Village India," *American Anthropologist*, Vol. 61, No. 5, Part I (October 1959), pp. 760-78; and also the following papers presented at the 59th Annual Meeting of the American Anthropological Association at Minneapolis, Minnesota, November 17, 1960: Gerald D. Berreman, *Caste and Economy in the Himalayan*

called the kisan-lagdar system. It is referred to hereafter as the farmer-retainer system. This system cuts vertically across the horizontal stratification of village society based upon caste. It does this on the basis of occupational considerations, and creates a pattern of relationships, still hierarchically organized, at the top of which stands the landowning farmer, generally a rajpūt. In descending order, determined by their caste status, are the various retainers who provide goods and services to that particular farmer. While the farmer exercises a considerable degree of authority over them, he has certain generally acknowledged responsibilities toward them. This pattern of economic organization has considerable importance for the nature of political action in the village, as we shall see shortly.

Every society, if it is to persist, must develop some mechanism for ordering the pattern of interaction between its members, both in the microcosm as well as the macrocosm.[3] The traditional pattern in which

---

Hills; Pauline M. Mahar, *The Hindu Jajmani System: The Paternalistic vs. The Exploitative Model*; William L. Rowe, *Economic Functions of Hindu Caste: The Jajmani System*.

[3] It may be of interest to consider, in this connection, the attempt by Almond to define a political system.

> ...(T)he political system is that system of interactions to be found in all independent societies which performs the functions of integration and adaption (both internally and vis-a-vis other societies) by means of the employment, or threat of employment, of more or less legitimate physical compulsion. The political system is the legitimate, order-maintaining or transforming system in society.

G.A. Almond and J.S. Coleman (eds.), *The Politics of the Developing Areas* (Princeton: Princeton University Press, 1960), p. 7.

the Indian village was related to the larger community for political purposes was through the headman, or small group of headmen. However, internally the problem of ordering the pattern of interaction between its members was far less uniform. In some villages the headman carried out this function. In others, and Khalapur is an example of this type, this function was carried out through the institution of the village panchayat. The term panchayat literally means a council of five, but has, however, been given a much broader usage, both in the literature dealing with village life in India, as well as by the villagers themselves. It is used to describe everything from an informal gathering called for a single occasion to the present-day formal permanent statutory institutions of local self-government. The notion of a panchayat, before the introduction of statutory bodies in the British period, was taken to mean any gathering of village leaders for the purpose of arriving at decisions. There was no sense of formal membership or fixed composition of such panchayats. Their composition varied with time and circumstance, reflecting at any given point the politically significant leadership in the village. The extent to which village panchayats existed in India, both in terms of their distribution throughout the country and the period of time during which they functioned, has been a subject of considerable controversy during recent years.[4] Most observers in

---

[4] For two statements of contrasting points of view on this matter see, H. D. Malaviya, *Village Panchayats in India* (New Delhi: All India Congress Committee, 1956), and Hugh Tinker, *The Foundations of Local Self-Government in India, Pakistan and Burma* (London: Athlone Press, 1954), and "Authority and Community in Village India," *Pacific Affairs*, Vol. 32, No. 4 (December 1959), pp. 354-75.

discussing the village panchayat, particularly as it is reputed to have functioned in the past, describe it as a single institution which functioned on a village-wide basis and exercised a monopoly over the decision-making process. The process of village government in Khalapur was carried on not by one, but several different types of panchayats. The sphere of competence of each type of panchayat was well defined by traditional practice. Each dealt with fairly distinct categories of problems. The sanctions which they could invoke differed in some instances to a significant degree. The fact that village government was carried on through a series of village panchayats rather than one single village panchayat may, in large measure, be due to the size of Khalapur.[5]

In any area an index of the degree to which a "modern" political system has penetrated is the extent to which the political process tends to be articulated and implemented through formal and legal structures, rather than informal, traditional ones based on kinship and status groups. While the former never completely supplant the latter, as a system moves toward modernity the dominance of traditional methods declines markedly.[6] Khalapur provides an interesting study in microcosm of a political system which has for decades fluctuated between the traditional and modern methods of articulation and implementation of the political process.

[5] Of the 1,642 inhabited towns and villages in Saharanpur District, only 11 had a population in excess of 5,000 in 1951. *Census of India, 1951, Uttar Pradesh, Part II-A-General Population Tables* by Rajeshwari Prasad, I.A.S., *Superintendent, Census Operations* (Allahabad: Superintendent, Printing and Stationery, Uttar Pradesh, 1952), pp. 25-6. All available evidence indicates that Khalapur has been one of the largest villages in the area for the past several hundred years.

[6] Almond and Coleman, *op. cit.*, pp. 9-25.

We can distinguish four distinct types of panchayats which were used in the traditional political process in Khalapur before independence. First, there is the caste panchayat; second, there is the general meeting panchayat; third, there is the farmer-retainer panchayat; and finally, there is, what for the lack of a better term may be called, the single purpose panchayat. All four were primarily adjudicatory in nature, and membership in each was based upon ascriptive characteristics. In 1920, and again in 1949, attempts were made to introduce throughout Uttar Pradesh panchayats set up under statute law with explicitly specified powers, duties and sources of revenue. While in both instances such panchayats were set up in Khalapur, the four traditional forms of village panchayat organization persisted, functioning parallel to the statutory panchayat. In fact, they have continued to operate down to the present day, and are still used to a considerable extent to regulate aspects of the internal village political process.

At least one caste panchayat exists for each caste in the village, and its jurisdiction extends to all members of that caste resident in the village. Its primary function is to uphold the pattern of social behaviour and the religious values of the members of that caste. It is also used to further the group interests of the caste. The panchayat itself is generally comprised of the leaders of each of the minimul lineage segments within that caste grouping. Within the dominant rajpūt caste this implies the leaders of each of the joint farm families, or groupings of each of the joint farm families in the village.[7] In some instances, particularly among the lower caste groups, one individual is recognized as the

[7] The term joint farm family will be explained further in Chapter II. For a fuller discussion of the concept of a joint farm family

leader of the caste panchayat. Regional groupings of these caste panchayats have existed in the past, and still do exist. The regional caste panchayat was called to settle a dispute which either could not be resolved within a single village, or which developed between the members of the same caste residing in two different villages. The penalties levied by these caste panchayats took the form of a reprimand, accompanied, perhaps, by a fine to be paid to the offended person or persons, or a feast to be given for the members of the caste. The ultimate sanction available to a caste panchayat—outcasting—implied the complete termination of all relationships with the offender by all members of his caste, his family included. In the past this generally was accompanied by banishment from the village. In times when caste rules were strictly enforced and all strangers were suspect, the threat of such a sanction had great force.

There is a considerable difference between the traditional regional caste panchayat and the contemporary caste association.[8] The former was primarily concerned with matters of religion and ritual, with the enforcement of caste rules and the adjudication of controversies concerning them. Its membership was determined by ascriptive characteristics, and it functioned in an ad hoc fashion. Among the lower castes these

---

and the role it plays in village political activity, see J. T. Hitchcock, *Dominant Caste Politics in a North Indian Village* (Berkeley: Center for South Asia Studies, February 1959), mimeo, *passim*.

[8] For a description of the contemporary caste associations see, Lloyd I. and Susanne H. Rudolph, "The Political Role of India's Caste Associations," *Pacific Affairs*, Vol. XXXIII, No. 1 (March 1960), and Selig S. Harrison, *India, The Most Dangerous Decades* (Princeton, New Jersey: Princeton University Press, 1960), pp. 96-136.

bodies were used in the attempt to alter the position of the caste in the ritual hierarchy, through what Srinivas has called "sanskritization."[9] The concerns of the contemporary caste associations are different. They are primarily directed toward socio-economic considerations, rather than with matters of religious orthodoxy or the position of their caste fellows in the local ritual hierarchy. The caste association seeks to improve the status of its members by gaining increased access to educational opportunities, government positions and other employment. In addition, their style of action is quite different. They act as lobbies or pressure groups on the local, district and State levels, and attempt to exert their influence on decision makers who are in elective office by making appeals to caste solidarity at the time of elections. Whereas the traditional regional caste panchayat was virtually a closed group, with no desire to recruit additional membership, the caste association eagerly accepts into its fold members of that particular caste group regardless of whether they come from the particular locality or not. One of the pressing needs is for scholarly enquiry into the origins of the caste associations and the degree of relationship in their formative stages with the traditional regional caste panchayats.

The general meeting type of panchayat, the second of the traditional types of panchayats, was concerned with the broad range of problems which would now be described as civil and criminal in nature. The membership of this panchayat consisted of the important leaders of each of the castes in the village. The size and composition of the general meeting panchayat varied

---

[9] M. N. Srinivas, "A Note on Sanskritization and Westernization," *Far Eastern Quarterly*, Vol. 15, No. 4 (August 1956), pp. 481-96.

directly with the nature of the problem before it. If a problem were sufficiently broad in scope and of marked importance, the panchayat might be attended by the leaders of each of the minimul lineage segments in each caste, and not just by one or two of the caste leaders, as would normally be the case. However, attendance and effective participation must be distinguished. From available evidence it is certain that these meetings have always been controlled by the members of the dominant caste in Khalapur, the rajpūts, and more precisely by the leadership group within that caste, i.e., the joint farm family leaders. The settlement of inter-caste disputes, or breaches of the peace and order, such as theft, were typical problems settled by this panchayat. The penalties levied by it were, in some instances, similar to those of the caste panchayat, i.e., fines, feasts to be given, etc. In addition, if a case involved disputed ownership of property, such as a bullock, the authority of the panchayat to award the property to one of the two contesting parties was recognized. The fact that the decisions of this panchayat, when arrived at, represented in effect the decisions of the leadership group within the dominant rajpūt caste in the village, added great weight to them.

The third traditional type of panchayat to be found in Khalapur is the farmer-retainer panchayat. Its composition is quite flexible and is tailored to meet the needs of the situation. In the village many problems arise which are of limited importance, both in terms of locale within the village and of the caste groups involved. We noted earlier that each individual participated in the farmer-retainer pattern of relationships. The retainers traditionally owed services to the land owning farmer and were rewarded at harvest time with a share of the produce.[10] The farmer, in addition to giving each retainer a fixed share of the harvest, had additional responsibilities towards them. Among these was his role as an arbitrator in the settlement of disputes in which they were involved and unable to settle among themselves.

Suppose, for example, a landless labourer of the chamar caste working for farmer *A* had a dispute with another member of his caste working for farmer *B*. They might first seek to have their chamar caste panchayat resolve their dispute. In the event that it was unable to do so, the two chamars would then approach the farmers for whom they worked and the farmers would call a panchayat, which would be joined perhaps by several other rajpūt farmers from the same residential area, as well as other members of the chamar caste from that area. Because of the integrated nature

---

[10] A land revenue record compiled during the British period for the village of Khalapur, the *Wazi-bul-arz*, dated 1867, set forth the following table of payments:

Caste	Occupation	Payment
barhāi	to make wooden implements for agriculture	1 seer* per maund† of grain produced
lohār	to make iron implements for agriculture	1 seer per maund
chamār	to look after cattle	1 seer per maund
naī	shaving and haircutting	1 seer per maund
kumhār	to make earthen pots and carry goods from one place to another	½ seer per maund
kahār	to supply water	1 seer per maund
dhobī	to wash clothes	½ seer per maund
bhangī	to sweep and clean filth	1 seer per maund

* A seer is 1/40th of a maund, and is equivalent to 2 and 2/35ths pounds.
† A maund is equivalent to 82 and 1/7th pounds.

of the economic system, and the virtual monopoly over the land held by them, the rajputs were able to effectively control the lower caste groups and enforce their decisions upon them. This could be done either by threatening to invoke certain economic sanction, as well as the less subtle but equally effective threat of physical force.

The fourth traditional type of panchayat which exists in Khalapur is what I have termed the single purpose panchayat. Under this category fall many of the inter-caste meetings of the village. There is little sense of permanence or continuity of membership, and they are generally composed of the leadership element of various participating castes. At these panchayats an attempt is generally made to arrive at some type of decision concerning a problem affecting the castes involved in the panchayat.

Available information indicates that prior to 1920, the four types of traditional panchayats collectively exercised a monopoly over the decision making process in Khalapur. The first and second types exercised the greatest authority in caste and non-caste matters respectively. All were self-contained units, drawing their authority very largely, if not entirely, from within the village situation, with few limitations on the scope of their activity. They were not democratic bodies in the present Western sense of the word. Their operations reflected the hierarchical nature of the social system, be it on an intra-caste or inter-caste basis, and in certain respects they are more accurately described as oligarchic bodies.

The decision making process in these panchayats is of particular significance since it contrasts sharply with that of the new statutory panchayats. This has become a focal point of criticism levelled by Jayaprakash Narayan and others, who feel that the newer panchayats, employing "Western" notions of democratic procedure, are fostering a spirit of divisiveness and faction, whereas the older, traditional panchayats conduced toward the development of village unity. In the traditional panchayat system the notion of voting for or against a particular proposition, with a majority carrying the issue and thereby binding the minority to that agreed decision, was and still is completely alien to the system. The normal method of decision making was to initiate consideration of a particular point in the panchayat and continue discussion until a consensus, satisfactory to all the significant groups in the panchayat, could be arrived at. In the event of a stand-off between several equally powerful groups in the village, discussion continued until it was obvious that no agreement would be possible. At that time the panchayat would be disbanded and an attempt would be made to reconvene a similar panchayat at a later stage, when either an alteration in the power status of the two groups involved had taken place or, for some other reason, a compromise seemed possible.

The "Western" notions of democratic procedure involve the possibility that a decision may be taken to which powerful elements in the village are strongly opposed. The problem of securing their cooperation in such a situation to implement panchayat decisions was something which the villagers had never encountered. By removing the need for consensus and placing a premium on securing a numerical majority, the newer systems in theory made it possible for the majority of the village to move ahead more rapidly in introducing reforms and changes without being held back by the more conservative elements in the village. The obvious difficulty was that these more conservative elements were the very ones who had the greatest interest in the preservation of the status quo.

The older panchayat system had been ideally suited to the needs of a tradition oriented leadership group which sought to minimize and control changes in the village scene. These older panchayats had, from the point of view of the traditional leaders, been effective units for the solution of village problems. The panchayat's sanctions were primarily religious, social and economic, though the element of physical coercion was not entirely absent. They functioned primarily as instruments for the settlement of disputes and the amelioration of conflicting interests. They were only to a minor extent concerned with any type of governmental activity other than the adjudicatory function. They were the institutional mechanisms through which the consensus of the village, on important issues, was developed and made manifest. That consensus, however, was largely shaped to reflect the interests of the dominant caste in the village, which, in numerical terms, was a minority of the total village community. The abrupt shock delivered to traditional village decision-making practices has thus been a twofold one. It has given the majority of the village community a potentially dominant voice in the decision-making process; and also, it has removed the necessity for that majority to carry the minority with it, or conversely, it has taken from the dominant minority, in theory, their ability to block the introduction of changes to which they are opposed.

It is for this reason that violence has on some occasions accompanied panchayat elections, in which members of sections of the village community, other than the leadership elements of the dominant caste group, have successfully contested village elections and sought to use the newer panchayats to alter village conditions. The traditional legitimate styles of political action have been done away with by a stroke of the legislative pen, but little has been done to condition the villagers to the acceptance of these new styles of political action.[11] One stratagem increasingly adopted by State Governments has been to place a premium on unanimity in elections and decision making. This has been an attempt to carry forward the old style of decision making into the newer institutional form. Its result has often been to enable the more conservative elements in the village to manipulate these new institutions to the continued service of their ends, to the detriment of other elements in the village community, while masking this action with the cover of legitimacy by utilizing the newer institutions for these purposes. The first village elections held in 1949 in Khalapur are, as we shall see, an excellent example of this point.

---

[11] For an interesting discussion of these problems see Susanne Hoeber Rudolph, " Consensus and Conflict in Indian Politics," *World Politics*, Vol. XIII, No. 3 (April 1961, pp. 385—399.

II
The Period of British Rule

IN 1803 Saharanpur and the other Districts in the Meerut Division of Uttar Pradesh were conquered by the British, and in 1805 certain British land revenue laws, known as the Oudh Code, which had been developed for nearby areas previously under British control, were extended to cover the areas in the Meerut Division, including Saharanpur District.[1]

At the outset the British were not concerned with problems of local self-government and therefore did nothing in a formal sense to disturb the traditional panchayat system. Their primary concerns were the maintenance of law and order and the collection of land revenue. However, the land revenue and police systems which they set up had an effect on the pattern of village government.

The period between 1805 and 1822 was marked by a gradual realization on the part of the British that the system of village organization and land holding in Saharanpur and the remaining Districts in the Meerut Division differed significantly from that in other areas under British control.[2] This realization culminated

[1] B. H. Baden-Powell, *Land System of British India* (Oxford: At the Clarendon Press, 1892), vol. II, pp. 13-15.

[2] The interested reader is referred to Baden-Powell's discussion of the problem. Briefly put, the British soon realized that the pattern of land ownership was quite unlike that in Bengal and Eastern Uttar Pradesh, i.e., the zamindari system, and also somewhat distinct from the ryotwari system of South India. It has generally come to be known as the mahalwari system and

in the passage of Regulation VII of 1822, incorporating various modifications which were gradually made in the Oudh Code, or those suggested due to the peculiarities noted in the areas. Regulation VII marks the creation of the office of *lambardar*.

The lambardar was a representative selected from the property-holding group within each separate area upon which land revenue was assessed. He was made responsible for the payment of the land revenue due from that area. This system was extended to Khalapur somewhere about the 1820's or 30's, and in the Wazibul-arz, dated 1867, a land revenue document for the village, there exists a fairly detailed statement of how this was put into effect, and of the individuals who were appointed as lambardars.

The land under control of the villagers in Khalapur was divided into ten mazras, a unit of land area for which a separate record of rights was maintained. Each mazra was in turn divided into two or more thōks. In each thōk there were several co-sharers, known as zamindars, and from among them a lambardar for the thōk was selected by the District Collector. In Khalapur each lambardar was responsible for several thoks, since for all ten mazras there were only eight lambardars.

---

displays several variations of a form of joint responsibility over, and rights in, the land which implied a status of equality between the several co-sharers in a particular area. A degree of confusion enters, in in that the term zamindar (or zemindar) is used in this system also, but in the mahalwari system it simply implies one who owns land, and who in most instances tilled it himself or through the use of hired labour or tenants. It does not imply the existence of a system marked by numerous intermediaries and absentee owners, between the tiller of the soil and its ultimate "owner," such as was common in the Bengal zamindari system. In Khalapur most zamindars tilled at least some of their land.

It was the lambardar's responsibility to see that the land revenue from each thōk was collected and deposited with the government.

In addition to their tasks as revenue collectors, the lambardars also functioned in an informal sense, as agents of the police. In the Wazi-bul-arz of Khalapur they were charged with the responsibility of seeing that no criminal or lawbreaker was allowed to remain in the village, and they were also responsible for maintaining the watch in the night.[3]

In introducing the office of lambardar into Khalapur the British had done little to disturb the traditional pattern in which the village governed its activities. All of the lambardars mentioned in the Wazi-bul-arz were rajpūts. All were large landholders, and from what we have been able to determine they were primarily members of the most important joint farm families within the village. The British had thus realized the threefold criteria of leadership which operated within the village at that time, i.e., caste status, extent of land ownership, and size of joint farm family. What they had done was to seek out the individuals who already held the positions of leadership and, in effect, enhanced their position by extending to them additional prestige as well as a portion of the State's police power. The significance of this is that we find leadership within the village deriving a portion of its authority from an external source.

While the office of lambardar was heritable, and normally was to pass to the oldest son of the incumbent,

---

[3] Of particular interest for our later discussion of village development activities is Section 10 of the Wazi-bul-arz, which stated: "...all expenses to be made in the village will be incurred by the lambardars, which they will then realize from the co-sharers."

provision was made for the removal of a lambardar. Thus,

> if a lambardar commits an offence, or is not good to the cultivators, the cultivators can make applications to the Collector for the removal of the lambardar from office. The Collector will record the evidence and if the allegations are proved, the lambardari will be terminated. Then the Collector will take the majority opinion of the co-sharers. If the votes for and against a lambardar are equally divided then the opinion of the Collector will be final.[4]

At the time of the land revenue settlement in the year 1887, there were eight lambardars in Kahalapur; seven were Hindu rajpūts and one was a Muslim rajpūt.

With the passage of time the lambardars became the main and almost the sole intermediaries between the village and the British administrative apparatus. Thus in times of economic distress it was they who approached the British and asked for a reduction or postponement in land revenue. In times of trouble or social unrest they were the individuals who were immediately contacted by the police and generally, upon their charge, villagers would be taken into custody or otherwise punished. As a result their position in the village was greatly enhanced, politically as well as socially. In addition, their role as interpreters between the villagers and the world outside, as represented primarily by the governmental apparatus, placed them in a unique position,

---

[4] Section 8, Wazi-bul-arz of Khalapur, 1867. It should be noted that there is no evidence to indicate that the removal power and the election of a new lambardar was ever exercised in Khalapur. Note also that the only people who would have participated in the election were the co-sharers.

able to influence the flow of information in both directions.

The growing importance of the lambardar tended to have an effect upon the panchayat system and its operation, particularly in the settlement of disputes. As one villager put it: "They were the men who did anything if there was anything to be done in the village." Thus, if a dispute occurred in the village it was considered to be their responsibility to settle it. The lambardars would call a general meeting panchayat or one of a more limited variety, depending upon the dispute or problem. At this panchayat, they would be largely responsible for seeing that a consensus was arrived at. "They would advise the people and try to bring about a compromise." When asked about the possibility of the interested parties not agreeing to the suggestions of the lambardars, the villagers quickly said that this could never happen, and that in any event this never did happen. "No one would disagree with the suggestions of the lambardars. They would advise the people and the people would do it."

In this fashion a pattern of action emerged in which a smaller group within the dominant caste rajpūt leadership group came to occupy an increasingly significant position in the village. No serious difficulties were raised, since they continued to follow the traditional legitimate forms for arriving at decisions and guiding village action; namely, the use of the panchayat and the stress upon consensus in decision-making. Their position of leadership was largely unchallenged by any source external to the group. Significant challenges did arise, however, from within the rajpūt caste group in the village, and for a fuller understanding of this it is necessary to consider certain aspects of the pattern of rajpūt social organization.

The rajpūts of Khalapur are a unilineal descent group, and, as Hitchcock points out,[5] a well established generalization of social anthropology in connection with such descent groups is the principle of structural relativity in their pattern of political action.

The politics of such a group is characterized by its invariable tendency towards fission and the opposition of its segments, and another characteristic is its tendency towards fusion with other groups of its own order in opposition to political segments larger than itself. Political values are thus always, structurally speaking, in conflict.[6]

The pattern of social and political organization among the rajpūts of Khalapur is exceedingly complex and does not conform to the notion of "factionalism" as seen by Oscar Lewis in his controversial study of Rampur, another North Indian village.[7] The group loyalties of the rajpūt caste group of Khalapur are most easily

---

[5] Hitchcock, *op. cit.*, p. 1. I am indebted to Hitchcock and my colleague Prof. John J. Gumperz for the information on which the following discussion of rajpūt social organization is based. Needless to say, I alone bear responsibility for the manner in which it has been interpreted and presented here.

[6] *Ibid.* See also, E. E. Evans-Pritchard, *The Nuer* (Oxford: at the Clarendon Press, 1940), and M. Fortes, "The Structure of Unilineal Descent Groups," *American Anthropologist*, Vol. 55 (1953), pp. 17-41.

[7] Oscar Lewis, *Group Dynamics in a North Indian Village* (New Delhi: Programme Evaluation Organization, Planning Commission, Government of India, 1954). A similar study equally controversial in its findings was carried out by one of Lewis' assistants on the Rampur project, Harwant Singh Dhillon, who has given us a study of factionalism in a South Indian Village. See, Government of India, Planning Commission, Programme Evaluation Organization, *Leadership and Groups in a South Indian Village* (Delhi: Manager of Publications, 1955).

The Period of British Rule

conceived of in terms of a series of concentric circles, decreasing in extent as they increase in intensity. Several of these "circles" relate the rajpūts of Khalapur to kinsmen outside the village, and Hitchcock identifies these as the caste, the *gotra*, the clan, and the *thamba*.[8]

Within the village, the largest circle is the entire village caste brotherhood. With few exceptions, the members of all 34 rajpūt lineages in the village are descendents of a common ancestor who acquired the village in about the sixteenth century. Generally speaking, each of these constituent lineages within the rajpūt caste group occupies a contiguous area within the compact village site. The entire village site is divided into seven distinct territorial subdivisions, which may be called boroughs (*pattis* in the local dialect). In each of these boroughs there is thus a grouping of lineage segments, which forms the second concentric circle of rajpūt loyalties within the village. The ultimate unit in this hierarchy is the joint farm family. The joint farm families are corporate groups in the sense that each owns land and property jointly, works the farm as a collective enterprise, and allocates authority to a single individual for representing it to the outside. It is what the anthropologist calls the effective minimul lineage, and what Hitchcock styles as the building block of the rajpūt political system.

A factor of utmost importance is the unambiguous authority of the male head. This man may depend upon another male, usually the eldest son, for the actual working and even the day to day management of the farm; and he has to depend upon his wife, or whoever is head of the women's house, for direction of affairs in that sphere. But ultimate authority

---
[8] Hitchcock, *op. cit.*, pp. 4-8.

rests with him, and in external affairs the social posture of the family is correctly regarded mainly as a reflection of his values and judgments.⁹

The individual lineages within a borough might be thought of as intermediate foci of loyalty between the borough, on the one hand, and the joint farm family on the other. Such lineages are generally styled an extended joint family grouping, and they do presumably play some structured role on certain types of ritual and ceremonial occasions, but the more important political unit intermediate between the borough and the joint farm family is the domain, which unlike the borough and the joint farm family may vary from time to time and is dependent on other considerations besides kinship, such as political and economic power. The principal manifestations of the characteristics of fission and fusion among unilinear descent groups, mentioned earlier, lies in the tendency among rajpūts to establish the intermediate units—styled domains—which at times even cross borough lines. In past centuries, while this could be accomplished by the individual grouping so inclined separating off and establishing a separate village, pressure on land forced the politically dynamic joint farm families to attempt to establish a domain through the process of fusion, forming alliances with similar groupings within the village itself. At any given time within the village one can discern certain ascendent and certain descendent domains. In the latter, one of the principal causes of decline is brought on by the process of fission, namely, a splitting up of the domain into its smaller constituent parts due to internal conflict, the death of the major leader without a commonly accepted successor, or some similar reason.

⁹ Hitchcock, *op. cit.*, p. 12.

What results from this is a continuously shifting pattern of alliances, and it is only by perceiving this fact aright that one can begin to understand the way in which political groupings within the village were able to form and re-form what at first might seem to be completely inexplicable, opportunistic alliances.

In their discussions of village political activity, the rajpūts themselves often referred to what they termed an ideal norm of village alliances. Although sometimes disregarded, it nevertheless formed an important consideration in the political action surrounding the second village election, as we shall see below. If, for example, an argument were to develop between a rajpūt of borough B and a rajpūt of borough D, it was felt by the villagers that the rajpūts of borough A would stand with those of B against D, while D could in turn expect to be supported by C, D and E. The latter group might also possibly be joined by F and G borough rajpūts. When the rajpūts of A and B boroughs stood together they were generally acknowledged by all to be superior to any combination of opponents possible within the village during the period up to 1947. Their leaders tended to exercise a monopoly over the important positions in the village. However, as we have earlier noted, it is the joint farm family which is the ultimate minimul lineage group, or political building block, and as such this ideal norm of alliances was, and still is, often violated. Groupings of joint farm families—domains— of one borough will support similar groups in another borough against other members of their own borough.

The villagers, in discussing group conflict within the rajpūt caste, acknowledge that there were three main sources of strife. These arose from disputes over the ownership or utilization of land; disputes over money lending and debts; and those arising from abuse of, or insult to, women. Of these three the most important by far was the first.

In developing the land around Khalapur, adequate access lanes or roads were rarely laid out, or if laid out were soon encroached upon. Thus, to get to his own fields a farmer often had to cross the fields of others. When he brought a plough and bullocks along damage often ensued to the standing crops in the fields crossed, thus laying the basis for argument and dispute. Sometimes a field left in fallow by one farmer was taken possession of by another, or perhaps its boundaries were moved to the latter's advantage. If a farmer had paid for 24 hours of irrigation water from the canal, another farmer, during the night, might alter the small irrigation channels that led to the fields for several hours, thus watering his fields at his neighbour's expense.

In many instances formal litigation in the courts established by the British ensured, and the sums expended often exceeded the initial amount in dispute. In these suits your friends gave evidence for you; your enemies against you, regardless of the fact that they may not have actually witnessed the particular event. The time-tested maxim of Indian politics, "the enemy of my enemy is my friend," was operative. If the position of one man in the village was particularly strong, his allies rather than he might be attacked. This resulted in an extremely complex pattern of alliances within the village. One principal and obvious effect of this was the extent to which these alliances retarded the possibility of joint action on the village-wide basis.

At the turn of the century several events occurred which had an effect on the pattern of village leadership and government. They stemmed from the passage of the United Provinces Land Revenue Act of 1901. Under the terms of this Act the area units of land revenue administration were redivided. This actually took place in Khalapur in 1907. Sixteen new units called mazras were created, and for each a lambardar was appointed, eight of whom were from A and B boroughs. In almost all instances the old lambardars continued on and the new lambardars were either from the same joint farm families or from other prominent rajpūt joint farm families in the village. There were no non-rajpūt lambardars.

At about the same time a new position was created by the British, that of mukhiyā. He was a member of the village appointed as an agent of the police, and as such exercised the powers which the lambardars had previously held in this respect. It was not possible to isolate the extent to which the creation of this position affected the status of the lambardars. The uncle of the new mukhiyā was one of the eight lambardars who held office prior to 1907, and at the outset, at least, little was done to disturb the prestige of the lambardars by the new mukhiyā.

The post of mukhiyā, as well as that of lambardar, had no direct relation, in the minds of the British who created it, to the internal village governmental system. It was conceived of as yet another instrument to make British rule more effective and efficient.

In 1920, as a result of the Montagu-Chelmsford reforms, certain "nation-building" subjects were transferred, at the Provincial level, from the control of the Governor and his Executive Council to popularly-elected ministries. Among these subjects was local self-government, and in a relatively brief space of time the United Provinces Legislature passed a village panchayat Act.[10] The statutory panchayats to be set up under the Act were, "...to assist in the administra-

[10] United Provinces Act, No. VI, of 1920.

tion of civil and criminal justice; and also to effect improvements in the sanitation and other common concerns of the village...."[11] Its members were appointed for a three year term by the Deputy Collector upon the recommendation of the leading villagers. Subject to good behaviour, they generally continued in office. Under the terms of the Act the size of the panchayat could vary from three to seven members—in Khalapur it was always six, five *panches* (judges or members) and one *sarpanch* (chief judge or head member). The panchayat was empowered to hear minor civil cases, where the property involved did not exceed Rs. 25 in value, and minor criminal cases under Sections 323 and 426 of the Indian Penal Code (assault and mischief). Its sole source of income came from the fines it levied, and it was empowered to spend the money thus raised for minor development works in the village. As we have seen, there were already in existence in Khalapur traditional methods for ordering village decision-making. Little consideration seems to have been given to the problem of how the statutory body would supplant the traditional ones, and what specific steps would aid in this process.

In addition to acting as petty courts, the statutory village panchayats were also charged with the responsibility of arranging for the improvement of primary education, public health, the supply of drinking water, the maintenance of village tracts, and works of public utility. These village development activities were to be financed from two sources: first from the fines and fees received by the panchayat in its judicial work, and second, from Provincial grants which were administered by the District Officer. While the judicial function of the new statutory panchayat was familiar to the

[11] *Ibid.*, Section 1.

villagers, the development function was an entirely new concept for them. Implicit in it was the notion of joint village action for the benefit of all residents of the village. This was something that simply had not been done in Khalapur.

As Tinker has pointed out in evaluating the success of these statutory panchayats, a great deal depended on who was elected as head of the village panchayat.

If a man of real standing in village affairs could be found to take up this responsible and onerous task, a substantial step towards success was taken. The ideal chairman must be a man of parts: he should come from a long established village family of repute to ensure respect; he should possess some education and experience of the outside world to talk back to officials and to adapt modern ideas on sanitation, agricultural improvement or schooling to the needs of his village; and he must be endowed with energy and with acknowledged personal integrity which would inspire the village folk to action, and cause them to accept his pronouncements without cavil. These are high requirements, and of course in many villages no such leader was forthcoming.[12]

Khalapur was fortunate in that, for a period of time, it was able to produce such a leader. In about the year 1915 the first mukhiyā in Khalapur died and a new one was appointed for the village. His name was Sucheet Singh, and it was with his appointment that there began to develop a new and different pattern of village leadership and action. Sucheet was a rajpūt, the head of a joint farm family which had in generations past succeeded in establishing the largest and most powerful domain

[12] Tinker, *op. cit.*, p. 205.

in borough *A*. This joint farm family controlled a thousand acres of land in the village and the surrounding area, and as such they were the largest landholders in Khalapur. By nature a quiet man, small of stature, he seemed to effect a revolutionary change in the thinking and actions of the village.

The list of Sucheet Singh's achievements in the field of village development are considerable. The most significant were the starting of a boys' primary school, the setting aside of a common village grazing ground for cattle, the construction of a major road within the village, the digging of four wells, the digging of a tank by the Sanskrit school and several other tanks within the village, and the building of the local Hindu temple.

One villager, in commenting on Sucheet Singh's achievements during his tenure as mukhiyā and sarpanch, pointed out, "What they now call *Shramdan* (voluntary labour, or gift of labour) was arranged in the village long ago by Sucheet." His methods were simple and direct, as witness the example of the digging of the tank by the Sanskrit school. A swami had urged Sucheet and other villagers to provide a tank for the school. Gradually interest in the project grew. Sucheet and the lambardars from the various boroughs exchanged views on an informal basis, and, realizing that there was considerable support for the project, Sucheet called a general meeting panchayat. The lambardars were responsible for seeing that all of the leaders from their respective boroughs attended. The merits of the project were then discussed and it was agreed that the tank should be dug. The total labour necessary to dig the tank was estimated and then portions allotted to each borough. The lambardars were each then given the responsibility of seeing that all of the people in their borough turned out on the allotted day to work, with Sucheet exercising general supervision. In this way the work was accomplished in a short space of time.

The simplicity of his method is deceiving, for this was a village long divided by group conflicts, and as villagers were prone to point out, prior to Sucheet's time there was little unity in the village. Some of the people recognized that the lambardars had the responsibility for carrying out works of general utility for the village along the lines indicated in Section 10 of the Wazi-bul-arz of 1867, but prior to Sucheet's time these works were not done. "Sucheet Singh was the first man to get the village to work together. Before that each man would do only those works which he was interested in getting done for himself and he would spend his own money on it." One major factor which seems to have contributed to Sucheet's success was an ability to rise above the conflicting group loyalties in the village and to establish a sense of public confidence based on a reputation for honesty and forthrightness. Of equal importance was the fact that he was the leader of the largest and most influential rajpūt domain in the village. It is quite clear from all available evidence that Sucheet was sustained in his position by a sense of public trust rather than by any economic or physical power of coercion available to him; however, he was not without enemies, and with the passage of time they finally succeeded in effectively challenging his leadership position.

When the statutory panchayat was created in the village in 1921, Sucheet was made its first sarpanch. The other panches of the panchayat were a brahman from B borough, a banyā from F borough, and three rajpūts from C, F and G boroughs respectively. This group continued to function under Sucheet's direction, with the exception of two replacements caused by the death of incumbents, until the time of his resignation in 1929.

The use made of this statutory panchayat during Sucheet's period as sarpanch was indeed an interesting one. It did not supplant the traditional village panchayat system; nor was it totally ignored by the villagers in favour of the traditional system. Rather it was incorporated in the traditional system and used as something akin to an appellate body. Few cases were actually recorded in the register of this panchayat. Many villagers pointed out that this was an indication of the strength and wisdom of Sucheet. In approaching the parties to a given dispute he would first seek, on an informal basis, to have them arrive at a compromise. If this failed he would then, if the case were of sufficient gravity, call a general meeting panchayat. At that time the parties to the case would be present, their positions explained, and the panchayat would generally give a decision. If one of the parties still felt that justice had not been done, Sucheet would then enter the case in the register so that official notice would be taken of it, and a meeting of the statutory panchayat would be called. While the terms of the Act of 1920 limited the jurisdiction of the statutory panchayat to civil cases, involving amounts not in excess of Rs. 25, under Sucheet cases involving thousands of rupees often came before it. Public confidence in his wisdom and impartiality was great, and justice was swift and inexpensive in his panchayat. His pattern of action reflected the villagers' preference for the traditional methods of decision making within the village. But where this method failed, Sucheet then availed himself of the statutory panchayat's additional coercive power, which derived from State law.

The two principal hindrances to the creation of village-wide unity in Khalapur were inter-caste and intra-caste conflict, which in each instance implied primary demands on individual loyalties. Sucheet Singh overcame these, and as a result he was able to bring about some joint village action for the purpose of improvement and development. He was respected not only by the rajpūts, his own caste members, but by all castes in the village.

Sucheet Singh became a member of the Arya Samaj, a Hindu reformist movement which for a time attained great strength in North India, and, as such, he began to attempt certain social reforms in the village. He tried to persuade people to stop drinking country liquor and to behave in a more acceptable and law-abiding fashion. Unfortunately he was unable to set his own house in order. A situation arose in which a member of a joint farm family within his domain persisted in acting in a manner contrary to the reforms which Sucheet espoused. This was clearly an act of defiance, and as such an indication that Sucheet had lost the support of a significant segment of the joint farm families which had previously supported him. As a result his leadership position was seriously compromised, and he therefore resigned from the posts of mukhiyā and sarpanch.

From available evidence it would seem that while one factor in his downfall was the opposition of many rajpūts to his Arya Samaj views, another, of even greater importance, was that his domain had made a number of enemies, particularly as it increased its landholdings at the expense of other rajpūt joint farm families in the village. In time the leaders of these joint farm families began to join together in opposition to him, harassing him through law suits in the British court system, and otherwise involving him in mounting debts and obligations. But the fusion that had taken place among the joint farm families opposing him was short lived, largely due to their failure to agree among themselves to the support of any given alternative domain leader for the position of village-wide leadership.

When Sucheet resigned from office, a rajpūt from borough *B* was named as sarpanch and mukhiyā by the Deputy Collector, upon the advice of Sucheet and several others in the village. It was obvious that this man was not an effective alternative to Sucheet, for almost immediately the prestige of the office declined and the new sarpanch was soon challenged by other groups of rajpūts who were successful in submitting a petition to the District Collector against him. When his term of office expired he was not renominated to the panchayat. However, he continued to hold the post of mukhiyā. A member of the same joint farm family as Sucheet Singh was then named to the post of sarpanch. In addition, due to the death of one member, a vacancy occurred and a chamār from a small settlement on the outskirts of Khalapur was also named to the panchayat. According to chamār and other untouchable leaders in Khalapur his appointment was merely a gesture by the government to the lower caste groups and in no way reflected any alteration in the power position of the rajpūts vis-a-vis the other caste groups. Within the rajpūt caste, however, it was apparent that following Sucheet, the representatives of no single domain had been able to gain hegemony over all others in the village, and there thus developed a stand-off between several competing groups. This was reflected in the fact that the leaders of the panchayat were unable to take any effective joint village action from the time of Sucheet's resignation down to 1947.

The third sarpanch, who had also been a member of Sucheet's joint farm family, continued in office until his death in 1939. While he enjoyed a somewhat better reputation than the second sarpanch, and was less partisan in his actions, he was unable to overcome the existing divisions in the village and establish his own hegemony. As such the statutory panchayat continued to lose favour and confidence.

Upon the death of the third sarpanch, his son, Gopal Singh, was appointed as the fourth sarpanch. Gopal was a relatively young man at the time, about 28 or 29, yet his nomination was accepted without question. This was largely due to the fact that he was well educated and extremely intelligent. During his father's term of office he had attended the meetings and had aided in keeping the registers; thus he was quite familiar with the panchayat proceedings. Soon, however, he too was accused of favouring certain groups within the village, and, in addition, of displaying strong pro-Congress sentiments. This was in 1942, when open anti-British agitation was in full swing, and his opponents, citing his pro-Congress sentiments, were able to have him removed from office. The villagers were finally able to compromise on a rajpūt from *D* borough, but it soon became apparent that he was a rather simple man who was unable to assert himself, and he was removed from office after only six months. His successor, who continued in office until the statutory panchayat was superceded by new legislation in the post-Independence period, was a member of one of the strongest rajpūt domains in *B* borough. During his tenure the statutory panchayat was rarely used.

The attempts by the British to introduce a statutory panchayat in Khalapur, although initially partially successful, ultimately resulted in failure. The inability of the statutory panchayat to completely supplant the traditional village decision-making institutions may be traced to a variety of factors, some stemming from the very nature of the new statutory body, others rooted more deeply in existing village conditions.

The factors inhibiting the functioning of the statutory panchayat in Khalapur, which were rooted in the very nature of the institution, have been commented on at length by Tinker.[13] The very newness of the institution was a factor working against it, since villagers tended to distrust that which was unknown and to continue to place their confidence in that which was known and had been proven successful. Another factor was that the use of the statutory panchayat involved certain formalities, such as payment of fees, and maintenance of ledgers and records. Its decisions did not necessarily have to be based upon a consensus of the various positions expressed in the course of a panchayat meeting, but rather could simply be the views of the group that had succeeded in controlling the majority of the positions on the panchayat. The very fact of a fixed membership implied that as power positions changed it would be difficult to reflect these directly in the composition of the body. In addition, the question of external supervision over internal village decisions was introduced. There was always the possibility that the District Officer might be successfully appealed to by one party or another to a given case, and the decision overturned. This was not the case with decisions of the traditional panchayats, where the award was not subject to any external review, save in the case of regional caste panchayats, and here the members of the caste group would at least be represented on that body.

[13] See Tinker, *op. cit.*, *passim*, for a thorough discussion of panchayat legislation in the period from 1921 to 1947.

Apart from those considerations which relate to the nature of the institution itself, there are the equally important considerations which stem from the existing village conditions, and more precisely from the fact that village political action was still controlled by the rajpūt oligarchy. The existence or absence of unity within that caste group largely determined the extent to which the village would effectively govern itself or lapse into a state of stagnation brought on by a stand-off between rival domains, each incapable of establishing its hegemony and thus bringing a semblance of unity to the village. None of the actions taken by the British had in any way seriously undermined the power position of the rajpūt oligarchy in the village. The introduction of the offices of mukhiyā, lambardar, and the positions on the panchayat of panch and sarpanch had at best tended to raise certain rajpūt leaders above the level of others, but this too had not represented any great alteration in status relations within the rajpūt caste group, since these posts tended to come under the control of those rajpūts who were heads of joint farm family groups which had established significant domains and had the support of numerous other joint farm families which, for the time being, cast in their lot with the domain leader. The inability of a group of these domain leaders in turn to unite and establish their hegemony over the village, guaranteed that village unity would not exist for purposes of village improvement and uplift, one of the underlying aims behind the introduction of the statutory panchayats by the British.

But even where such unity existed, due to effective leadership within the village, there was still much that was required before the development and uplift of the village could be brought about. The village leaders had to be capable of developing an awareness of the need for improvement and articulating the demands of the villagers as they developed. It was largely on their interest, enthusiasm and support that the initial success or failure in these ventures depended. They also often depended upon the existence of funds, plans and competent technical supervisory personnel. This implied some degree of help from sources external to the village, and during the period from 1921 to 1947 such help had to come, if at all, from the District Officer. Under men like Braine and Darling in the Punjab, local institutions and development activities experienced considerable success, but this was the exception rather than the rule.

In the face of all these obstacles it is little wonder that the statutory panchayat failed to gain a secure place in the village decision-making process in Khalapur, and to carry out the purposes for which it had been intended during this period.

III
The Introduction of Panchayat Raj

WITH the advent of Independence the new government of the United Provinces began work on legislation which it hoped would "revitalize the corporate life of the village communities and transform them into an effective instrument for rural improvement."[1] The local self-governing bodies provided for in the United Provinces Panchayat Raj Act, 1947, differed in several significant respects from those created under the Act of 1920. First, the judicial and administrative functions of the panchayats were separated and two distinct bodies were created to handle these functions. Second, the powers, duties and financial resources of each of these bodies were, in theory at least, significantly enhanced. Third, the system of selection of their members was drastically revised. Nomination was rejected and direct election with complete adult suffrage was adopted. Fourth, an administrative hierarchy exercising detailed powers of guidance, supervision and review over the village bodies was created at the Tahsil, District and State levels. Finally, at a later date, the powers of the village administrative bodies were further increased due to the passage of two pieces of land reform legislation by the State Government, each of which called for the utilization of the gaon panchayat, the administrative

[1] Statement of Objects and Reasons, U.P. Panchayat Raj Act, U.P. Gazette Extraordinary, cited in S. M. Husain, *U.P. Panchayat Raj Act* (Lucknow: Eastern Book Co, 1955), 2nd ed., p. 1.

panchayat, in the implementation of certain of their provisions.

The two types of village government bodies created by the Panchayat Raj Act of 1947 were the gaon panchayat, an administrative panchayat, and the adalat panchayat (later renamed the nyaya panchayat), a judicial panchayat. The extent of jurisdiction of a gaon panchayat was generally one village (save in those instances of very small villages which might either be joined together or linked to a larger village). Its membership, varying from 30 to 52, depending upon the population of the village, was directly elected. In Khalapur the membership of the first gaon panchayat was 52. The adalat panchayat's jurisdiction extended to from three to five gaon panchayat areas, and would thus normally cover five or six villages. In this respect it differed markedly from the previous panchayats in that now men would sit and hear cases involving people from villages other than their own. An individual bench would consist of five members and the benches would be rotated.

In addition, the Act provides for the selection, by direct village-wide election, of a village *pradhan* (president), whose primary function is that of chief administrator, and as such, he presides over the meetings of the gaon panchayat. An *up-pradhan* (vice-president) is elected by the members of the gaon panchayat from amongst their number.

The terms of office of the members of the gaon and adalat panchayats, and the pradhan, are all five years, with the proviso of a one year extension of their terms at the discretion of the State Government. The up-pradhan serves for one year and then in theory reverts to his normal status of member of the gaon panchayat, whereupon either he or another man is elected as up-pradhan for another one year term.

The area of jurisdiction of each gaon panchayat is established as a body corporate by the State, and styled a gaon sabha. It is given the power to acquire, hold, administer and transfer property, both movable and immovable, and to enter into contracts, sue and be sued.[2]

The gaon panchayat is charged with a series of obligatory duties and functions which include: construction, repair, maintenance, cleaning and lighting of public streets; medical relief; sanitation; regulating the construction of a new building; assisting the development of agriculture, commerce and industry; the administration of civil and criminal justice; the construction and maintenance of public wells; and, the care and management of the common grazing grounds.[3] It is also empowered to carry out certain discretionary functions, among which are included: assisting and advising agriculturists in the obtaining of government loans, development of co-operation, and establishment of improved seed and implement stores. The Act creates a gaon fund and empowers the gaon sabha to borrow money, to levy and collect taxes and to receive such fees as are legally due it.[4]

Since the main interest of this study is in an analysis of the non-judicial aspects of village government, further discussion of its judicial function, now handled by a separate body, the adalat panchayat, will be omitted, save in those instances where it or its officers directly affected the pradhan and the gaon panchayat.

This brief review should serve to indicate that the

---

[2] Article 4, U.P. Panchayat Raj Act, 1947, as amended.

[3] See Appendix A for a complete listing of the obligatory as well as discretionary functions of the administrative panchayats.

[4] See Appendix B for a list of the tax schedules and the types of fees which could be levied by the gaon sabhas.

Government of Uttar Pradesh put its desire for the gaon and adalat panchayats to act as instruments for the revitalization of village corporate life into effect by giving to them an impressive series of powers, as well as enhanced sources of revenue. In so doing, however, they had created a lengthy and complex statute. As amended, the Act contains some 114 Articles, as well as 250 detailed Rules and numerous tables and charts. The annotated copy before me runs into some 132 pages, not including the index. In the light of this fact it should not be too surprising that several of its basic provisions, let alone minor details, were neither understood nor even known by the villagers and members of the gaon panchayat in Khalapur. While some effort had been made by officials of the Panchayat Raj Department to explain the Act to the villagers, it was clear that this effort had been, at best, a limited success. Further, in connection with government literature designed to explain the Act, it is necessary to remember that the dialect of Hindi spoken in this area differed to some extent from the highly Sanskritized official Hindi in which Uttar Pradesh Government documents are drafted.[5]

The passage of the Uttar Pradesh Zamindari Abolition and Land Reforms Act of 1950 and the Uttar Pradesh Consolidation of Holdings Act of 1953, added additional powers and duties to those of the pradhan and the gaon panchayat. The Zamindari Abolition Act stipulated that for each separate village there would be created

---

[5] For the problems which this difference in dialect raises, the reader is referred to the article by John J. Gumperz, "Language Problems in the Rural Development of North India," *Journal of Asian Studies*, Vol. 16, No. 2 (Feb. 1957), pp. 251-9. Professor Gumperz was a member of the same research project as the author, thus his conclusions are directly applicable.

The Introduction of Panchayat Raj

a body corporate known as the gaon samaj. Its membership would consist of all the adults who ordinarily resided in the area for which it was established. All uncultivated land, forests, fisheries, etc., not included in private holdings, became the property of the samaj. The gaon panchayat was charged with the responsibility of establishing a committee which includes all the members of the gaon panchayat, with the pradhan as its chairman, to be known as the Land Management Committee. This Committee was charged with duties relating to the supervision and management of the gaon samaj lands. The money received by the gaon panchayat Land Management Committee in this capacity is credited to the gaon fund. As we shall see below, the power of the Land Management Committee included the sale of village lands and orchards, a situation which introduced serious temptations for both village officials and residents.[6]

In 1953 the Uttar Pradesh Government passed the Consolidation of Holdings Act for the purpose of eliminating, as far as possible, fragmented land holdings. In order to implement the purposes of the Act, a part of the Land Management Committee, created under the Zamindari Abolition and Land Reforms Act of 1951, was constituted as the Land Consolidation Committee and was charged with the responsibility of advising the Assistant Consolidation Officer, the administrative official in charge of implementation of the Act at the village level, with respect to information concerning village lands. Its principal officers were often called as

---

[6] For a discussion of some of the problems which arose from the creation of the Land Management Committees see *Report of the U.P. Panchayat Raj Amendment Act Committee* (Lucknow: Superintendent, Printing and Stationery, U. P. [India], 1954), pp. 14-18.

witnesses in cases of partition, transfer, or disputed ownership of land holdings which could not be settled due to inaccuracies or omissions in the land records. The oral evidence offered by the members of the Land Consolidation Committee, particularly the pradhan, in many instances was the deciding factor in a case.[7]

In both of the instances cited above, in the Land Management Committee and the Land Consolidation Committee, the members of the gaon panchayat and the pradhan were drawn into participation, *in an official capacity*, with local problems of land ownership, utilization, transfer, etc., a subject which has long been the principal cause of disputes, particularly within the dominant rajpūt caste. The results of this involvement, as we shall see shortly, damaged the effectiveness of the gaon panchayat and the pradhan of Khalapur.

News of the impending change in the structure of village government came to the villagers, as does most other news, in a gradual fashion, through a variety of sources, each presenting a slightly different interpretation of the facts in question. For some of the villagers the local land revenue officer, the *patwari* (*lekhapal*), was the first to bring the news; for others a knowledge of the impending change did not come until the officers of the Panchayat Raj Department visited the village. Another source of information was the Member of the State Legislative Assembly, from that constituency, who

[7] In cases involving disputed ownership of land holdings a somewhat more rigorous system of review obtained. Evidence was submitted to the Assistant Consolidation Officer and the decision was made thereon by an Arbitrator, usually located at District Headquarters. By removing title cases from the village it was hoped that impartiality would be insured, but the decisions were still to be made upon evidence and testimony, and where written evidence of title was inconclusive, the oral testimony of the pradhan would carry much weight.

visited Khalapur and delivered a speech explaining the law and its benefits. Upon one thing, however, all villagers are agreed—as soon as the knowledge of the impending changes in village government came to be known, "everyone started trying to pull things to his own side."

The greatest interest centered in the office of pradhan. There was virtually no dispute and even little interest in how the gaon panchayat would be constituted. The rajpūts, who comprised 41 per cent of the population, were aware that in the event of an election for the post of pradhan they lacked the necessary votes to carry the day, particularly if the other caste groups in the village formed an alliance against them. This, in fact, was what began to happen. The lower castes realized that if they joined together there was a chance for them to wrest control of village government from the rajpūts. Gradually a lower caste or non-rajpūt party began to develop. Its principal leaders came from many of the castes in the village, i.e., a banyā, a barhāī, two brahmans, three chamārs, a jatiya chamār, a bhangī, a kumhār, a lohār, and a bharbhuja. In addition, several rajpūts joined with the lower caste group to oppose the major rajpūt grouping. Most prominent among these was the rajpūt from *B* borough, who had been the second sarpanch and mukhiyā from 1929 to 1931 under the Panchayat Act of 1920. The principal candidates under consideration by this group for the post of pradhan were a brahman and a baniyā.

The rajpūts, increasingly aware of their "minority" position, decided that their only chance for victory lay in breaking the united non-rajpūt front, and they proceeded to try to win the brahmans to their side. While numerically speaking this would still have only represented 47 per cent of the village population, in the popular understanding, a rajpūt-brahman alliance could not be beaten. The rajpūts thus decided to support a brahman rather than one of their own number in the belief that they would be able to select one that they could control. A fear entertained by many of the rajpūts was that one of their own number might well prove to be more difficult to handle if he should decide to embark on an independent course. Initially the names of four brahmans were under consideration by the rajpūts. It soon became known that two of them were members of the non-rajpūt party and obviously acceptable to it, thus rendering them unacceptable to the rajpūts. Therefore, one of the two remaining brahmans under consideration was approached by the rajpūt leaders. He pleaded ill health and an advanced age, suggesting to the group that they choose someone else. He put forward the name of the other brahman, who was still acceptable to the rajpūt group. This man had heretofore been virtually inactive in village politics, and possessed few discernible characteristics of leadership. One day prior to election day he was approached and agreed to become the candidate of the rajpūt-brahman alliance. Those brahmans who had been active in the non-rajpūt party were then under obligation to split off from it and support their own caste member. The remaining members of the non-rajpūt party, which by this time had come to be called the labour (*mazdūr*) party, were furious.

On election day several officials of the Panchayat Raj Department came to the village and a general meeting panchayat was called. Up to this time the villagers had given little consideration to the selection of members of the gaon and adalat panchayats. They were told of the number of vacancies on each of the two panchayats and it was strongly suggested to them that in constituting the gaon panchayat the census of the village be taken into consideration. By this it was implied that each caste grouping should be given some representation on the panchayat, roughly in accordance with its population in the village. (The list of members of the first panchayat and their caste membership closely parallels the percentage breakdown of village population by caste.) The first step taken was to decide how many seats would be allotted to each of the seven boroughs in the village, and then within that how many would be allotted to the rajpūts. At this point a leading rajpūt from each of the boroughs was called upon to suggest the names of the rajpūts from his borough who would be nominated. Then a member of the banyā caste was asked to suggest the names of the members of the remaining castes, other than the untouchables, to fill in the seats proportionally allotted to them. Finally, the untouchables were asked to propose the names of candidates to fill the seats reserved under the law for them. The total number of seats thus having been allotted, the names were then put forward in a bloc and an unanimous election was declared. (In a similar manner the members of the adalat panchayat for Khalapur were chosen.)

The name of the brahman, supported by the rajpūts, was then proposed for pradhan and passed without open dissent. However, feeling was still running high, particularly against the brahmans who were held to be responsible for the entire turn of events. As soon as the election was completed, members of the mazdūr party arose and announced that henceforth none of their group would perform the traditional services for the brahmans. There were some reports that they had held a panchayat among themselves prior to the election, when it was apparent that the brahman supported by the rajputs would be selected pradhan. At that time it was agreed to boycott the brahmans with the added threat of a fine of Rupees 150 being levied on any caste group which broke the boycott. It was difficult to document this exactly, but most observers agreed that there had been a fine involved in the boycott decision.

Accounts of the length of the boycott varied from several days to several months. In a sense all were correct. The bhangīs (sweepers), whose services were required on a daily basis, soon capitulated under rajpūt pressure, but the other groups whose services were given less frequently and were of a less essential nature were able to hold out for a much longer period of time. A group of rajputs who soon became the leading supporters of the new pradhan went to the various castes and with a mixture of threats and persuasion attempted to get them to resume their services for the brahmans. Some months after the election an event transpired which served to finally break the boycott. A bullock belonging to one of the brahmans died, near the brahman's house. Word was sent to the jatiya chamārs requesting that they come and perform their traditional service of carrying away the carcass of the animal and disposing of it. They refused. The animal continued to lie where it was for several days in the warm sun, becoming more objectionable daily. A group of the rajpūts went to them and on the one hand offered to pay any fine which might be levied, and on the other, threatened them with an immediate beating if they failed to comply with the brahman's request. The jatiya chamārs yielded and removed the carcass, but no fine was levied. Soon after, all the remaining groups capitulated and began performing their traditional services for the brahmans. It should also be remembered that under the farmer-retainer system the performance of services was a reciprocal matter and as such the brahmans had refused to officiate at all the various rites and ceremonies in which the lower caste groups would have been involved. As with all strikes, both sides were affected.

In regard to the election, two points should be noted before proceeding further.

(1) Despite the widespread opposition to the brahman pradhan and his rajpūt supporters, no one at the time of election stood forward to cast a vote against him, and it was recorded as an unanimous decision. Thus, attempts to grade the powers of panchayats according to whether or not they were unanimously elected, a move suggested by some, would, in this case at least, have been carried out on the basis of a complete mis-reading of the situation. The support and confidence implied by an unanimous election, which officially took place in this case, did not exist.

(2) Voting was done by an open show of hands rather than by secret ballot. This was definitely an inhibiting factor. Still it was felt by many that this election had been decided by the traditional method of arriving at village decisions. In this traditional method alternative decisions are considered and discussed at length, with the merits and demerits of each proposal fully and publicly explored. Gradually a consensus emerges in support of that one of the several alternatives which is most acceptable to all. At no time is there a vote with the majority view carrying over the minority opposition. In its ideal form there remains no opposition, for all have been convinced of the wisdom and necessity of the particular decision. In the election of the brahman pradhan some of the form, but certainly

none of the substance of this traditional method, had been utilized. However, this was sufficient for many villagers, particularly the rajpūts, to look back upon it at a later stage and praise it as being in conformance with "the good old way." They compared it critically with the actual election contest which developed at the time of the second elections.

For several weeks after the election the pradhan, with the aid of several of the rajpūt members of the gaon panchayat, began to form a series of sub-committees, each charged with the supervision of a particular substantive area of the gaon panchayat's total jurisdiction, i.e., an Education Committee, a Health and Sanitation Committee, etc. The panchayat and its committees, as thus constituted, represented a fair cross section of the traditional leadership of all of the castes in the village. Virtually all the men selected were leaders of their joint farm family and/or caste groupings. Generally speaking, they were advanced in age and many, particularly the lower caste members, were illiterate. Few members outside the rajpūt group had ever exercised political power in the village or had ever participated in village decision-making. The rajpūts constituted the largest single membership bloc and at the outset they maintained a semblance of unity, though this was to prove short-lived. Little had been done to alter the economic dependence of the lower castes on the rajpūts, and as the final breakup of the brahman boycott had shown, even a united bloc of lower castes would eventually have to yield.[8] The

---

[8] Another example of the ability of the rajpūts to meet opposition and beat it was the strike of the landless agricultural labourers for an increase in their monthly wages. The incident took place several years earlier. At that time the landless labourers in Khalapur were receiving a wage of Rs. 25 per month, about

only effective challenge to rajpūt power could come from within that group and this was what developed as the gaon panchayat began to function.

Rs. 5 below that paid in the villages of the surrounding area. They tried to persuade the rajpūts to raise their wages but met with no success. Finally, all else failing, they decided to refuse to work for the rajpūts—literally to go on strike. They felt that the rajpūts would soon require their services to care for and harvest the crops and would thus have to capitulate, for it would be almost impossible to bring in sufficient labour from the outside during the harvest season. But the rajpūts remained adamant and proceeded to play their trump card—control of the land. Many of the landless labourers kept a cow or an oxen and thus required fodder. Heretofore they had been allowed access to the fields to gather it. Now this access was denied them. In a like manner, permission to seek fuel and other necessary daily items was also denied. Faced with the possible loss of their cattle, their most valuable possession, the landless labourers gave in and returned to work. In all, the strike lasted for less than a week. No such action was tried again. In this connection it should also be noted that a most important "by-product" of the Zamindari Abolition Act was the provision which insured to all the ownership of the dwelling in which they resided, and the land it occupied. Previously the house and land of the landless labourers had been the property of the rajpūt farmers, who did not hesitate to evict an uncooperative labourer.

IV

The Functioning of the First Gaon Panchayat

IN July 1949 the gaon panchayat of Khalapur began to function. The initial phase of its activities revealed several interesting conditions which were to affect its future operation and potential success. Among these were the weakness of its leadership under the brahman pradhan; the lack of a clear understanding by the members of the statutory powers and duties of the gaon panchayat; and, their irregular pattern of participation in the functioning of the gaon panchayat. None of these taken separately posed an insuperable barrier to the successful operation of the body; still the net result was to render it ineffective.

The weakness of its leadership is revealed in an analysis of the initial resolutions passed and the action taken on them. One problem which had long troubled the village was the illicit manufacture and consumption of country liquor, an alcoholic beverage made from fermented sugar cane. Relatively inexpensive, it accounted for much of the drunkenness in the village. In the meetings of March 11 and 14, 1949, the gaon panchayat passed a series of resolutions prohibiting the sale or consumption of country liquor in the village. It held that anyone found drinking it would be fined Rs. 25 to Rs. 50, and that anyone found selling it would be fined Rs. 100. At the first of these two meetings 26 of the 53 members of the gaon panchayat were present, and at the second 20. The bulk of the attendance was drawn from (1) rajpūts from A and B boroughs, (2) from untouchables, and (3) a few members of the artisan castes. Conspicuous by their absence were many, if not all, of the rajpūt members from the other boroughs.

The next mention of the question arose over a year later at the meeting of August 14, 1950. The action of the panchayat in the intervening period had little effect and it was decided, therefore, to appoint a committee to enforce the resolutions. The committee consisted of two rajpūts from A borough, two rajpūts from B borough, and three untouchables. The inability of this group to enforce the initial resolutions was reflected in a later resolution passed by the panchayat which represented a retreat from its initial position. It merely censured those who sold country liquor without stipulating any punishment, and piously said, "... the drinker can keep only one bottle of liquor, not more."

The panchayat had chosen extremely unpopular ground for one of its initial tests of strength. Many of the rajpūts of the village drank country liquor, and among them were included several of the influential leaders in the village. The resolutions of censure, while passed without opposition, were far from representing the unanimous decision of the full membership of the gaon panchayat.

The Panchayat Raj Act is silent on the subject of prohibition. However, it might be interpreted that the authority to legislate on such a subject is contained in Clause (p) of Articles 16, Discretionary Functions of gaon panchayats, which authorized a panchayat to make provision for "... any other measure of public utility calculated to promote the moral and material well being or convenience of the villagers." The lack of a clear directive to undertake this type of action seems to underscore the questionable value of a village body engaging in an attempt to adopt prohibition. The failure to obtain the complete support of all the rajpūt groups within the village was indicative of the dubious nature of its potential success. Further, this marked an initial split which was later to manifest itself into a complete disintegration of the rajpūts' "united front," which had made possible the election of the brahman pradhan.

In the development of the health and sanitation of a village one of the most important initial measures to be undertaken is the provision for the effective disposal of sewage and other waste materials. These materials are often removed from houses by means of drains which empty out on to the village lanes, creating an unsanitary condition and providing a breeding ground for mosquitoes. The gaon panchayat, in accordance with provisions of the Act, as another of its initial measures, passed a resolution requiring each house owner to prepare a soak pit, according to specifications, which would provide for the sanitary disposal of the sewage. A fine of Rs. 10 for non-compliance was authorized, in addition to which, in such cases, the panchayat was empowered to proceed with the construction of the soak pits and to charge the cost to the respective house-owners. During the entire term of office of this panchayat few soak pits were dug in Khalapur. Apart from one or two further resolutions passed by the panchayat which restated the original resolution, no further official action was taken.

One aspect of this issue which requires consideration is the extent to which the impetus for constructing soak pits had come from within the village, rather than being

The Functioning of the First Gaon Panchayat

suggested by outsiders, such as the Panchayat Secretary, upon the prompting of the Panchayat Raj Officer in Tahsil Headquarters. Evidence obtained by the writer did not show that the villagers themselves desired the soak pits, nor were they even convinced of their utility. The drainage problem at the home of the pradhan, for example, remained as objectionable as any in the village. It was evident that the passage of this, as well as several other similar resolutions, was done to satisfy requests and promptings by officials external to the village. The officials from the Tahsil Headquarters had contented themselves with the passage of the resolutions, feeling that the problem of its implementation was up to the villagers.[1] The net effect was that the gaon panchayat passed resolutions which did not reflect the felt needs of the villagers. The subsequent lack of follow-up and prodding by the officials led to a loss of prestige by the gaon panchayat in regard to this phase of its operations. It passed resolutions, but did not implement them. It threatened sanctions, but did not put them into effect.

A second problem which hindered the success of the gaon panchayat in Khalapur was a lack of understanding by the majority of its members of all of the powers available to them and the range of the duties they were required to fulfill. This problem became most pointed at a later date in regard to the ability of the members to control and/or depose the pradhan for malfeasance. However, an initial manifestation of this is found in the assumption of judicial functions by the gaon panchayat, which were properly the subject for consideration and

---

[1] This will be dealt with at length below. To this writer one of the most serious shortcomings of the programme has been the emphasis placed upon conformance to procedural "niceties" rather than what might be termed substantive or operative aspects of performance.

action of the adalat panchayat at a time when the latter body was operating effectively.

The earliest records of the gaon panchayat, dating from its commencement in 1949, list the receipt of applications filed by villagers who presented claims or charges against other villagers which were clearly the subject of minor civil and criminal cases and thus within the jurisdiction of the adalat panchayat. A typical case was one which involved a chamār, an untouchable landless labourer, who was accused of uprooting gram plants from a field of a rajpūt. Testimony of witnesses was taken, and after the accused admitted guilt the case was reported as settled by mutual compromise. Other cases heard involved assault, robbery, nonpayment of debts, damage to standing crops, etc. In many instances one or both of the parties was an untouchable. Cases involving members of the artisan castes and the rajpūt caste were less frequent. One exception to this related to the rajpūts of B borough. They filed several cases concerning encroachment on common grazing ground, the breakage of water canals for irrigation, and other minor cases of theft or damage to standing crops. Since these men were among the group of rajpūts who were close to the pradhan, and could normally expect him to be favourably disposed to them, this is not surprising.

An exception to this pattern occurred among the last cases to be heard by the gaon panchayat. In this instance one of the rajpūts from B borough was accused of breaking irrigation canals by a group of the most powerful rajpūts from F and G boroughs. The accused agreed to refrain from such action in the future and the case was resolved by mutual compromise. Soon after the above-mentioned case the gaon panchayat ceased to act as a judicial body. This was indicative of the stalemate which developed between rajpūt groups in the village.

In explaining to the writer why the gaon panchayat was utilized as a judicial body, when this was clearly not the intent of the government, the villagers simply shrugged and stated that there were times when it was felt that it would be better to bring a case before it rather than before the adalat panchayat.

The irregular pattern of participation of the members is largely explained by the fact that:

1. A desire for active continuous participation did not exist. As long as things were going well for the rajpūts they were not too concerned. The other caste groups were unfamiliar with a role in decision-making and did not attempt to push themselves. "After all," they would say, "it was a rajpūt panchayat—what could we do?"

2. The pradhan soon developed a circle of close associates. Many meetings were poorly announced and held at his home rather than in a public place. Afterwards the register would be sent to several illiterate untouchable members who would mark it (by thumb print), signifying they had attended when, in fact, they had not. The pradhan and his "cronies" were often the only ones to attend. A quorum, required under the Act, was the exception rather than the rule.

3. In those few instances when important decisions were taken, i.e., land allotment, most of the leadership group attended, but otherwise inaction on the part of the panchayat led to poor participation by many of the members.

The total period of operation of the first gaon panchayat in Khalapur extends from August 1949 to April 1956, a span of six years and nine months. It evolved in a series of distinct phases: the first, characterized by an unfamiliarity with the institution and its powers;

the second, by a heightened awareness of its potentiality by a limited group which attempted to achieve a measure of personal gain as a result of it; and the last, by a stalemate between opposing groups in the village. Perhaps the best way to approach the topic is through a review of the fiscal activities of the panchayat. In an analysis of the collection and disbursal of funds we are led into the various ramifications of the gaon panchayat's operation.

Article 13 of the Act provides that "an annual estimate of income and expenditure" for the following year, for each gaon sabha (the village body corporate) will be passed by it at a meeting to be held each autumn (*kharif* meeting), and a review of the accounts for the preceding year will be made at its Spring meeting (*rabi* meeting). Provision is made for the times of the meetings to be altered so long as they are held on a semi-annual basis. Through these meetings the gaon sabha was expected to exercise fiscal control over the gaon panchayat, its administrative agent. This would be accomplished since the pradhan and the members of the gaon panchayat would be greatly outnumbered in such an assembly of the village electorate. However, it would be only reasonable to assume that the pradhan and the members of the gaon panchayat would play a leading role in the formulation of the budget, and of the various programmes to which it would give effect.

On August 18, 1949, at a meeting in which 41 of its 53 members were present, the gaon panchayat drafted a budget of Rs. 2,150, to cover the period of 15 August 1949 to 31 March 1950.[2] On August 23, 1949, a meeting of the gaon sabha was held which approximately

[2] Itemized breakdowns of the budgets of 1949-50, 1950-51 and 1951-52 were not available. However, according to the pradhan they were virtually identical to the budget of 1952-53,

550 persons attended. At that time the budget, as prepared by the gaon panchayat, was passed without dissent. Later, on September 19 of that year, a meeting of the gaon panchayat was held at which time a proposed schedule of taxation was passed, in a series of by-laws, to raise the revenue for the proposed outlays in the budget. The tax list thus prepared represented an effective coverage of the itinerant merchants and many, but not all, of the occupations practised in the village. Most significant by its absence was any tax schedule covering either agriculturists, which would have hit the rajpūts, who own 90 per cent of the cultivable land in the village, or a tax which would cover the brahmans. The group heaviest hit when the actual levies were made were the banyās (merchants). The pradhan was appointed tax collector.

TABLE I
GAON SABHA BUDGET: 1952-53

Income	Rs.		Rs.
Professional Tax	400	Panchayat Management	440
House Tax	1,500	Education	440
Licence Fees	100	Medical Treatment	220
Adalat Panchayat	120	Community Construction	440
Other	80	Public Health	220
Total	2,200	Adalat Panchayat	110
		Previous Expenditure	110
		Balance	220
		Total	2,200

The estimate of income from taxation was roughly 90 per cent of the total anticipated income of the gaon for which an itemized breakdown is available (see Table I), and which was the same in total outlay as the 1950-51 and 1951-52 budgets, differing only by Rs. 50 from that of 1949-50.

panchayat. The remainder was expected to come from fines levied by the adalat panchayat and other unidentified sources. Thus nine-tenths of the burden of village government was to be borne directly by the members of castes other than brahmans and rajpūts.

The budget outlined in Table I, above, differs in one respect from that of the year 1949-50 inasmuch as a house tax was not sanctioned by the gaon sabha until the following year, i.e., 1950-51. The main sources of income for the year 1949-50 were to be licence fees and the occupational or professional tax.

For each year of its operation a budget was passed which outlined the proposed sources of income as well as the planned expenditures. These were prepared under the guidance of the Panchayat Secretary, an official of the Panchayat Raj Department, and the financial plan thus prepared was forwarded annually, through channels, to the District Panchayat Raj Officer for consideration and approval. It did not bear even a faint resemblance to what went on in terms of actual fiscal activity. Tables II and III list the actual income and expenditure of the gaon sabha for the entire period of operation of the first gaon panchayat. A review of these figures will give us a much better indication of just how the pradhan and the gaon panchayat progressed.

In its first fiscal period, from August 1949 to March 1950, the actual receipts were Rs. 595-7-6, of which Rs. 10 came from a gift and the remainder from taxes and licence fees levied in the village. A review of the individual receipt registers from which the figures in Tables II and III were reconstructed reveals that the major tax revenues came from the merchant caste, with weavers, oilmen, and cobblers and other untouchables comprising the bulk of the remainder.

TABLE II

INCOME OF THE GAON PANCHAYAT

Period	Taxes & Fees	Gifts	House Tax and Sale of Land	Adalat Panchayat	Government Grants	Other	Total	Cumulative Total
Aug. 1949 to March 1950	585/7/6	10/—/-	—	—	—	—	595/7/6	595/7/6
April 1950 to March 1951	311/—/-	32/—/-	—	20/4/6	150/—/-	60/—/-	573/4/6	1,168/12/-
April 1951 to March 1952	38/—/-	100/—/-	—	30/—/-	—	—	168/—/-	1,336/12/-
April 1952 to March 1953	58/4/-	54/—/-	—	—	—	592/—/-	704/4/-	2,041/—/-
April 1953 to March 1954	—	193/12/-	3,272/8/-	—	350/—/-	11/4/9	3,827/8/9	5,868/8/9
April 1954 to March 1955	6/—/-	33/—/-	2/8/-	—	500/—/-	443/13/-	985/5/-	6,853/13/9
April 1955 to Feb. 1956	—	—	—	—	—	100/—/-	100/—/-	6,953/13/9
TOTAL	998/11/6	422/12/0	3,275/—/-	50/4/6	1,000/—/-	1,207/1/-	6,953/13/9	

TABLE III

EXPENDITURE OF THE GAON PANCHAYAT

Period	Salaries	Panchayat Magazine, Stationery & Incidental Expenditure	Kisan Inter College*	Cattle	Construction of Panchayat-Ghar	Total	Cummulative Total
Aug. 1949 to March 1950	24/11/-	—	—	—	—	24/11/-	24/11/-
April 1950 to March 1951	113/5/6	280/9/-	400/—/-	8/—/-	31/—/-	832/14/6	857/9/6
April 1951 to March 1952	98/—/-	43/13/3	—	—	29/2/-	170/15/3	1,028/8/9
April 1952 to March 1953	64/—/-	32/15/6-	—	—	792/14/9	889/14/3	1,919/7/-
April 1953 to March 1954	73/—/-	130/2/6	700/—/-	60/—/-	3,257/14/3	4,239/—/9	6,157/7/9
April 1954 to March 1955	22/—/-	16/15/-	—	5/—/-	813/10/3	857/9/3	7,015/1/-
April 1955 to March 1956	22/—/-	80/14/-	—	—	—	102/14/-	7,117/15/-
TOTAL	417/—/6	585/5/3	1,100/—/-	73/—/-	4,942/9/3	7,117/15/-	

* Local agricultural secondary school. Items listed here were gifts to it made by the gaon panchayat.

The Functioning of the First Gaon Panchayat   73

One of the numerous administrative forms which the gaon panchayat had to maintain, under the terms of the Act, was a tax list of the village which contained the name, residence, taxable income, amount of annual rent, and the amount of tax payable for all villagers subject to taxation. The register was maintained after a fashion, but again it too bears little resemblance to the actual taxes levied. The collection of taxes by the pradhan was an extremely sporadic affair, marked by alternating periods of calm and intense activity. It had little pattern to it save for a very effective initial coverage of the merchant caste, the banyās.

As shown in Table II, the net receipts through taxation and licence fees levied in the first fiscal period, August 1949 to March 1950, represented the largest amount gathered through this method by the gaon panchayat in any one fiscal period during its entire term of office. While it falls far short of the estimated Rs. 2,000 set forth in the annual budget, it serves nonetheless to demonstrate the extent of availability of funds in the village which might be raised for development purposes. One source of taxation listed in the Act, which would serve to supplement handsomely the professional and licence fees, is a tax on the amount of land revenue paid by the agriculturist to the government.[3] If this source were effectively tapped, and all

[3] In subsequent years the gaon sabha passed an authorization to levy a tax on land revenue, but at about that time plans were developing to build an agricultural secondary school in Khalapur. The major subscribers in the village were the rajpūts, who paid a variety of taxes to support this project, i.e., a tax of Rs. 30 per plough from all agriculturists; a tax of Rs. 30 per annum to be deducted from the amounts to be paid by the sugar mills to the cultivators for their cane crops. These funds, however, were not handled by the pradhan and the gaon panchayat, but by a special school committee set up by the villagers. At that

other levies were uniformly and regularly made, there would have been little difficulty in making up the total planned income.

The reluctance of the community to levy taxes directly upon itself in any great magnitude is typical, but it should be noted that where the villagers were persuaded of the value of a project to be carried out and of its necessity, funds were soon forthcoming to support it. The construction of the agricultural secondary school (see footnote 3, p. 74) is a case in point. It should also be noted that during the entire first fiscal period of the gaon panchayat's operation the net disbursements were in the amount of Rs. 24-11-0, paid in salary to the Panchayat Secretary; whereas the receipts were Rs. 595-7-6. No development or other public works were planned or initiated. To the average villager, during this period, money was going in but none was coming out. When this was coupled with the growing rumours that the pradhan was engaging in chicanery in the collection of taxes, public confidence and support began to wane. Since the interests of the rajpūt group, which exercised an effective monopoly of political power in the village, were largely unaffected nothing was done to alter the situation in a direct fashion. An indirect approach to the problem, at a later date, was the creation of the separate school construction committee, largely staffed by rajpūts, and a similar committee for the paving of the village lanes.

During its second year of operation the receipts from taxation decreased, notwithstanding the fact that a new tax, a house tax, had been authorized by the gaon panchayat under the guidance of the pradhan and his supporters. Under Section 224 of the Rules appended to the Act, panchayats are authorized to levy a tax on

---

time trust and confidence in the formal institution of local self-government was rapidly diminishing.

houses and buildings not to exceed 5 per cent of their annual rental value. A substantial portion of the taxes assessed in this year were under this new authorization. Through it the pradhan got to many of the lower caste members who were not taxed in the first year. A review of the pradhan's receipt books reveals that apart from a few "repeaters," mostly banyās, taxation in actual practice was pretty much a one-shot affair. Having paid their tax to the panchayat, most villagers felt that this was enough. They should not be taxed again.

The net yield through taxation declined progressively, and in the last three years of its operation a total of only six rupees was gathered, and this, as indicated in the records, covered back taxes for the two previous years, as well as the tax for 1953-54. The use of taxation as a source of revenue to finance village development work and general public works came to a virtual standstill. There are several reasons for this. First, in order to enforce any programme of taxation the pradhan needed the approval and active support of the leadership of the village, i.e., the rajpūts. This he had gradually lost, due partly to internal splits within that group, as well as the passage by the gaon panchayat of unpopular resolutions, such as the prohibition resolutions, which tended to alienate segments of the rajpūts. In addition, the rumours of the pradhan's misuse of gaon sabha funds, as well as charges of illegal activity in connection with his position as tax collector, grew and tended to gain widespread acceptance. Equally important is the fact that midway through its term of office funds became available to the gaon sabha through other sources,[4] thus relieving the pressure to use further

---

[4] Funds became available through the sale of village lands under the terms of the U. P. Zamindari Abolition and Land Reforms Act, 1950, to be discussed below.

taxation as a means of raising revenue to support the public works projects that had been embarked upon. In this manner a valuable potential source of revenue for further public works fell into disuse.

The major, and in fact the sole, public construction which the gaon panchayat embarked upon in its first term of office was a panchayat *ghar*—a village community hall—a project which accounted for 69 per cent of its total expenditures. Construction began in March 1951 and extended over a five year period, ending in 1955. It was difficult to determine to what extent the idea for the construction of a panchayat *ghar* originated in the village, and to what extent it was due to the prompting of outside officials. The fact that it is now a source of pride to the village leaders who display it to all who visit the village makes an unbiased account of its origins difficult to ascertain. However, since there are several notations in the records made by Panchayat Raj Department officials reminding the gaon panchayat that the panchayat *ghar* was to be a model for the entire Tahsil, and numerous urgings to hurry its completion, there is some reason to suspect that this was initiated upon prompting from outside. Completion of the construction of the panchayat *ghar* depended upon the realization of a new source of revenue, since direct taxation had proven insufficient over the long run. The funds became available to the village as a result of the passage of the Uttar Pradesh Zamindari Abolition and Land Reforms Act of 1950.

In addition to the creation of institutions of local self-government in the village, another of the major reforms which the Uttar Pradesh Government embarked upon in the post-Independence period was land reform. It resulted in the passage of legislation to abolish absentee landownership and to insure that title would vest, to the greatest extent possible, in the tiller of the soil. Under the terms of Part II, Chapter 7 of the Uttar Pradesh Zamindari Abolition and Land Reforms Act, 1950, provision was made whereby all cultivable and uncultivable farm land—ponds, tanks, groves, forests, etc.—not comprised in private holdings would vest in a corporate village body to be known as the gaon samaj. The gaon panchayat was to be the administrative agent charged with the "superintendence, management and control" of gaon samaj lands. The gaon panchayat was therefore directed to establish a committee to be known as the Land Management Committee, which was to consist for the time being of all the members of the gaon panchayat and to be headed by the pradhan.

The total land area controlled by the villagers of Khalapur was about 9,600 *bighas* (6,000 acres). Of this, 500 *bighas* were vested in the gaon samaj at the time of its creation in 1953, and of the last figure, roughly 270 *bighas* were cultivable fallow land.

In addition to its task of superintendence, management and control of the 500 *bighas* of village lands, the Land Management Committee was charged with a series of additional functions in respect of all village lands, including those in private holdings. These functions included: the development and improvement of agriculture; the maintenance and development of the *abadi* site (residential area of the village) and village communications; the development of co-operative farming; the consolidation of holdings; and, the development of cottage industries.[5]

[5] Article 118, U.P. Zamindari Abolition and Land Reforms Act, 1950, as amended. Chapter XI of the Act gives further instructions and details concerning the implementation of proposals relating to collective farming, and the incentives,

The thing which interested the villagers most was the provision for the disposal, through sale or tenancy arrangements, of the cultivable fallow lands in the village that were not in private holdings. How village lands would be allotted, and to whom, became a matter of interest and some dispute. Under the terms of the Act[6] preference was to be given in admitting people to gaon samaj lands in the following order: (1) educational institutions, for a purpose connected with instruction in agriculture, horticulture or animal husbandry; (2) a landless agricultural labourer; (3) a farmer who owns less that $6\frac{1}{4}$ acres of land (about 10 *bighas*) in the gaon samaj area; (4) a co-operative farm; and (5) any other person. Since a good bit of the cultivable fallow land held by the gaon samaj lay close to the village and was thus extremely useful to agriculturists, the manoeuvering became quite intense.

The gaon panchayat, in its capacity as the Land Management Committee, finally passed a resolution stipulating that the land of the gaon samaj would be sold to those cultivators "...who are able to utilise the land properly, at the price of Rs. 200 per *bigha*." The obvious intent of the resolution was to make the rajpūts eligible to acquire land. Since a landless labourer would not be able to pay Rs. 200 per *bigha*, they were rather effectively ruled out of consideration. (However, it should be noted that one chamār was able to purchase

---

such as reduction in land revenue, which will apply. No one in Khalapur formed or attempted to form a collective farm, and there is no evidence to indicate that the Land Management Committee carried out any activities in this respect. Later attempts have been directed to popularizing co-operative farms, but this too has had no effect on Khalapur.

[6] Article 198, Clauses (i-a) through (d).

a plot 3½ yards wide by 7 yards long adjacent to his home for the price of Rs. 10.)

Virtually all of the land sales were to rajpūts. The largest single area sold was only about 2 *bighas*, and most were only ⅓ to ½ *bigha*. The total amount of land actually sold amounted to between 10 and 15 *bighas*, or between 6 and 9½ acres. In addition, about 100 *bighas* (about 62 acres) was let out to *asamis* (literally tenants) of the gaon samaj, who turned out to be mostly rajpūts. On balance, neither the land area nor the amount of money involved were of any great magnitude, but the trouble and damage that ensued as a result of these transactions by the pradhan and the gaon panchayat was considerable.

A problem immediately arose in that there were several claimants for each plot of land to be allotted. No matter what decision was made, some were bound to be dissatisfied, and charges of favouritism and corruption inevitably arose. (It might be added that in most, if not all, instances these charges of favouritism were not entirely without foundation.) In some instances the persons who sought a particular plot of land were involved in long-standing disputes. The act of allocating the plot to one of these parties tended to draw the pradhan into the network of disputes. Thus the pradhan was soon involved quite deeply in the quarrels of the rajpūts. Whereas previously his actions had not tended to affect the rajpūts to any marked degree, now they were directly involved and the pradhan became the focus of much of the old group conflict and bitterness.

The more disgruntled rajpūts decided to take action. Before the year was out a petition was filed in the Tahsil Headquarters against the pradhan. The complaint in the petition did not directly involve the allotment of land. It was concerned with some of the orchards in the village. Permission had been granted by the pradhan in the name of the Land Management Committee to cut some of the trees in an orchard, when in fact such an action was contrary to the provisions of the Uttar Pradesh Zamindari Abolition and Land Reforms Act. The pradhan was enjoined from carrying out further activities on behalf of the Land Management Committee pending a complete review of the matter. Up to the end of his term in office no further action was taken, and the net effect of the petition was to halt further sale or lease of village lands.

Several references have been made above to the charges that the pradhan had been engaged in chicanery.[7] Toward the end of his term in office, in an interview with the writer, the pradhan commented that if a pradhan so desired it might be possible for him to collect some panchayat taxes without issuing any receipts. The implication of his remark was clear. He went on to defend his administration, saying that he had always tried to use his office to please the people in the village. He had acted according to "village rules and not State laws." He offered several examples of instances in which the land allotments which had been made had gone to people whose holdings exceeded the $6\frac{1}{4}$ acres maximum area stipulated in the Uttar Pradesh Zamindari Abolition and Land Reforms Act. In other instances he certified people as rightful tenants (asamis) of village fallow lands when in fact they were not. To his dismay he had been able to please no one. "They were my friends until their selfish ends were fulfilled."

[7] The pradhan died shortly after the completion of his first term in office. The inclusion of the following information is not meant to malign him in any way. Rather it is my hope to demonstrate clearly the effects of transferring to the panchayats, at a relatively early stage, certain powers over village lands.

The pradhan's opponents claimed that there were several additional ways in which he was able to satisfy the demands of his supporters for the spoils of office. The most prevalent, as noted above, was in connection with giving receipts for taxes which he had collected. In some instances he was dealing with people who knew nothing of the regulations, save for the fact that they were being asked by the pradhan to pay taxes. They realized that they were under some obligation to do so. After receiving their taxes the pradhan, it was charged, either gave no receipt, or if one was demanded gave a receipt for less than the amount. If the taxpayer was illiterate, the matter was closed. If he could read he would be told that the receipt just given was for that part of the amount necessary to register the tax (say a receipt of Rs. 1 instead of Rs. 10), and that a receipt for the balance would be forthcoming after the tax payment was registered in Tahsil Headquarters.

Receipts were also to be given for all other transactions, such as land transactions, but as one villager put it: "What do I care if I get a 'chit' for Rs. 50 when I have paid Rs. 500, as long as the land is now mine. That is the important thing." If the balance went into the pradhan's pocket, as some people claimed, it did not seem to matter too much.

The Uttar Pradesh Zamindari Abolition and Land Reforms Act placed certain restrictions on cutting trees down—mainly fruit-bearing trees in orchards or groves. Sometimes a woodcutter or woodseller from another town would contact a villager in Khalapur and negotiate for the sale of an orchard. Certification by the pradhan that the trees involved were not fruit-bearing was necessary. The pradhan's opponents charged that it was generally given for a consideration amounting to 10 per cent of the sale price of the orchard to be paid by the woodcutter.

It is interesting to note that in discussing the above matters with the writer, the officials in the lower echelons of the Land Revenue Department were not at all unfamiliar with the manner in which the pradhan had supposedly manipulated his powers in regard to village lands and profited thereby. These officials were in direct and constant contact with the villagers throughout the Tahsil. They recounted numerous instances quite similar to those mentioned above. The net impression was that the main area of difficulty, which had embroiled the panchayats in village disputes and had resulted in corrupt activity, arose from the extension of powers of land management and control over certain village lands to them.

A third major piece of legislation passed by the Uttar Pradesh State Government, aimed at revitalizing the village communities, was the Uttar Pradesh Consolidation of Holdings Act of 1953. In addition to absentee ownership of land, another problem which plagued villagers has been the fragmentation of land holdings. The Act, as passed, superseded the U.P. Consolidation of Holdings Act of 1939 and portions of the U.P. Zamindari Abolition and Land Reforms Act of 1950, both of which provided machinery for the voluntary consolidation of land holdings by the villagers themselves.

In 1952 the villagers had tried to carry out a voluntary programme of land consolidation in Khalapur. At a general meeting panchayat, attended by the Tahsildar, a land Revenue Department officer, the villagers agreed to form committees in each of the seven boroughs. Each committee was to be responsible for consolidating land holdings of the people of that borough. Immediate difficulties were encountered since the land holdings of

Khalapur villagers are distributed in ten separate mazras,[8] and while the residents of one borough might hold a majority of the land in the mazra contiguous to it, they also held land in other mazras rather far removed. In addition, the land of the area is of varying quality, and each separate quality of land (of which there are about ten) has a different tax rate. If land quality B has half the tax rate of land quality A, it does not follow that two acres of B equal one of A. As the villagers proceeded the administrative and procedural difficulties increased.

It was decided that the consolidation should be carried out borough-wise. An attempt was made to consolidate the holdings of villagers in F borough in a mazra contiguous to it. All the lands in this mazra belonged to five rajpūt domains—joint farm family clusters—residing in F borough. These five domains were on relatively amicable relations. The land also happened to be fairly uniform in character, and after some time the work of consolidation in this mazra was completed.

In the second borough to attempt consolidation, the proceedings soon broke down. Strong competitive groupings existed within the borough. The qualities of the land concerned were many and, in addition, two

---

[8] The reader will remember that a mazra is an area for which a separate record of rights is maintained by the Land Revenue Department. The area of the smallest of the ten mazras was 304 acres, while that of the largest was 2,375 acres. The total area was about 6,000 acres. The complexity of the problem might be further under-scored by pointing out that in this area there were 11,204 separate plots. The land consolidation officials later determined that there were 5,520 corrections which had to be made in the records, which ranged from minor corrections on the land map to changing the name of the person recorded as owner of a plot.

of the members of the committee tried to engage in sharp practices. Voluntary consent to the proceedings was required of a majority of the landholders in the area concerned, and this was not forthcoming. As a result of this failure the entire voluntary proceedings were abandoned.

The passage of the Act of 1953 marked the beginning of the compulsory proceedings. An administrative organization was set up by the State Government to implement the Act, and while every effort was made by the staff of the Consolidation Department to get the voluntary consent of the villagers to the consolidation schemes, this was no longer an absolute necessity. The pradhan and the gaon panchayat were drawn into the proceedings, since the Land Management Committee, created under the Uttar Pradesh Zamindari Abolition and Land Reforms Act of 1950 (which consisted of the pradhan and the members of the gaon panchayat), formed the main source from which members were drawn to staff the Consolidation Committee which was to aid the State officials in the processs of land consolidation.

A major difference between the Consolidation Committee and the Land Management Committee was that the former functioned solely as an advisory body. It had no powers of direction, supervision or control over land given to it. The administration of the programme in the village was directly under the control of the Assistant Consolidation Officer, who was responsible for virtually all decisions made in connection with the programme. Appeals from his decisions were allowed, but these were to higher authorities. The extent of possible involvement of the pradhan and the gaon panchayat in controversies over land rights was limited. The main function of the Consolidation Committee was to supply information and advice concerning the village lands and their use. The Act specifically directed the Assistant Consolidation Officer to seek the advice of the members of the Consolidation Committee on such matters as soil classification. The only area in which the Consolidation Committee could have become directly involved in factional quarrels related to the judicial functions of the Assistant Consolidation Officer.

In addition to his administrative duties, the Assistant Consolidation Officer also functioned as a judicial officer. He entertained petitions for the amalgamation or partition of holdings and, in addition, in a case of disputed ownership, he took evidence and testimony. This data was then forwarded to a regular judicial officer, specifically designated as an Arbitrator, who had the sole power of decision in such cases. In a case involving disputed ownership the testimony of the Consolidation Committee, and particularly of the pradhan, might be crucial in the event of an obvious error or omission in the formal land records regarding a disputed plot.

The Assistant Consolidation Officer of the Khalapur circle was an honest and effective individual who was able to control the situation by talking privately to the parties concerned, and seeking out information from villagers who had no direct interest in a particular case. In this way he was able to keep down the number of cases filed. In the total land area of 6,000 acres, involving 11,204 separate plots, where 5,520 mistakes had been detected in the land records, maps, etc., only 51 cases were filed, and of these 50 were settled in the village, largely by mutual consent and compromise. Thus the work of consolidation, as carried out under the compulsory programme, did not involve the panchayat in Khalapur in further factional troubles. Credit here, as noted above, is due largely to the Assistant Consolidation Officer stationed there.

It will be remembered that in the discussion of the old panchayat systems which functioned prior to the passage of the Act of 1920, the extent of outside supervision, direction and control was minimul. Contact was made with the village leadership elements for the purposes of revenue collection, but apart from that village government was solely in the hands of the villagers, and its action or inaction reflected directly their desires. With the advent of the statutory panchayats, particularly since Independence, the institutions of village government have become increasingly subject to external pressures generated by a variety of agencies and individuals. The concern of these agencies has been largely connected with the economic development of the village community and the raising of the standard of living of its inhabitants.

Deference to authority in a formal sense, while retaining a freedom of action in substantive matters, or as the Report of the Reserve Bank of India's Rural Credit Survey has termed it: ". . . the illusion of implementation woven round the reality of non-compliance," is a pattern of action long followed by the villagers, and one which they have yet to discard to any significant degree. This attitude has complicated their relationship with many of these external bodies, and in some instances has frustrated the good intentions of the external agent. An excellent case in point would be the relationship between the gaon panchayat and the Panchayat Raj Department officials who were to give guidance and encouragement to the villagers and aid them in developing institutions of local self-government. Among the many registers and logs which the gaon panchayat was required to maintain was an "Inspection Register" in which official comments on the panchayat's activities were recorded. On occasion official comment was recorded directly in other registers, such as the "Agenda Register," etc. A review of these inspection notes indicated the extent to which "higher authority" tended to fall into step with the pattern of action, or should I say evasion, practised by the villagers. The bulk of these entries are concerned with matters of procedure. For example, one entry reads: "The Tax List register for 1951 has not been properly maintained. The information in this register should be complete at all times. This action should be accomplished immediately."

In another instance the monthly meeting log contained a record that the budget had been proposed, but the following meeting did not indicate clearly its passage, only that it had been introduced at that meeting. A notation was made by the inspecting officer that the budget should be formally passed. Even a casual perusal of the record book involved would have provided ample indication that the gaon panchayat of Khalapur was at that very time a moribund body. Most of the meetings were attended by ten or fifteen members of a total of fifty-three. The real intent of the Act, to build up corporate village spirit, was thus lost sight of by the officials in the process of demanding compliance to procedural niceties.

In reviewing the work of panchayats and attempting to measure their success or failure, the primary indices used by the Panchayat Raj Department were statistical in nature, i.e., how many miles of village lanes were constructed, how many soak pits and wells were dug, how many panchayat ghars were constructed, etc. This approach is reflected in virtually all literature dealing with panchayats. It should not be surprising therefore to find that the lower echelon officials concerned themselves with completing forms signifying such progress almost to the exclusion of any work really conducive to developing a spirit of self-reliance and initiative in the villages. When it was necessary to display such "recorded" progress to a touring official, numerous lower echelon officials converged upon the village and urged on the completion of a particular project. Construction activity in Khalapur varied directly with the coming of an important visitor, and the work proceeded in fits and starts marked by relatively long periods of inaction. (This was in direct contrast with another village observed, where village leadership was relatively cohesive and a spirit of self-reliance and local initiative seemed to have developed. There, work on pavement of village lanes, for example, proceeded at a uniform pace under the sole guidance of local village leaders.)

The net effect of the activities of the Community Development Programme officials in the area closely paralleled that of the Panchayat Raj Department. In both instances the officials understandably laid emphasis on those aspects of the programme which could be visibly demonstrated. They were much less interested in precisely how it was accomplished. The respective officials of each of the two departments with whom the villagers were in direct and fairly constant contact were the Village Level Worker and the Panchayat Secretary. The impression given by both men was that their major interest was in supporting and engaging in efforts, the result of which could be readily shown to their superiors. Further, due to their relative youth, inexperience and lack of official power, they were in no position to make a direct approach to the problem of building unity within the village, and thereby resuscitating its elusive "ancient corporate spirit."

To the extent that others, not of the village, tended to become involved in village politics and factionalism, the effect of their action was to further divide rather than unite the villagers. The main example here is that of the Principal of the secondary school built by the villagers. As long as the Principal's activities remained primarily concerned with securing "an extra share of the development pie" for the villagers he was accepted. His attempts to control the selection of the pradhan at the second election (to be discussed below) soon placed him in direct opposition to the groups opposing "his candidate," and for a time his ability to remain in the village was in doubt. He has remained, but his effectiveness, at last report, was seriously diminished. The Principal's ties with extra-village groups were primarily with the Congress Party.

It is interesting to note that the Principal's efforts to implement District Congress Party policy, when coupled with his own ad hoc intervention in village politics, resulted in the creation of a substantial and open anti-Congress sentiment which previously had not existed. To one research worker he had commented that the village was divided and that its people needed someone to come in from the outside and lead them, a person of strong character. There was little doubt as to who in his mind most appropriately fit the bill. It seems never to have occurred to him to attempt to find a ground for reconciliation of the major conflicting groups in the village, with a view toward creating a stable, permanent spirit of co-operative action, such as had existed under the old sarpanch, Sucheet Singh.

V

The Election of the Second Gaon Panchayat

As the second panchayat elections drew near the prestige of the pradhan and the gaon panchayat were at a low ebb. Most of the villagers professed ignorance of the provisions of the Panchayat Raj Act, which would have enabled them to impeach the pradhan. The few who showed any awareness of these provisions felt that what had been done was sufficient. In the new election they would see to it that the old pradhan was not chosen again. The rajputs particularly were willing to settle for *status quo ante bellum*, since under it they were quite capable of protecting their own interests. To most other groups inaction largely meant an assurance of no further taxation and to them this was an acceptable situation. There was no strong demand within the village for a change in its past pattern of leadership, characterized by formal or informal rajput dominance.

The rajputs were not willing to entrust the post of pradhan to a non-rajput once again. Most of them stressed the fact that they had gravely underestimated the powers which were given to the pradhan under the law. They maintained that such an office must be held by a rajput. The non-rajput opposition was silent, but watchful. It had not forgotten its failure in the first elections, and its leaders were reluctant to repeat it.

The Election of the Second Gaon Panchayat

Interest in the coming elections centered largely on the post of pradhan, as it had in the first election. While no one was eager to openly announce his candidacy, it became known that at least one rajpūt from each of the boroughs was canvassing the village for support. No member of the brahman or artisan castes was openly campaigning, though many villagers feared that the old pradhan would seek re-election. Mention was also made of an untouchable candidate, though in the early stages few paid much attention to this.

It would be helpful at this point to outline the basic procedural aspects of the pre-election period, set down in the Panchayat Raj Act, for in the weeks that followed they played a significant part in shaping the character of political action. First, within a specified period of time all persons desirous of contesting the post of pradhan, gaon panchayat member, or adalat panchayat member were required to obtain nomination papers from the officials in Tahsil Headquarters. A small fee was charged for these nomination papers. On a date designated by the Panchayat Raj Department, and posted in the village, all candidates were required to file their nomination papers with a Returning Officer who came to Khalapur. The names of all candidates were then posted for public scrutiny, and on the following day provision was made for questioning or challenging a candidate's eligibility. Ten days were set aside in which candidates were given the opportunity to withdraw their nomination papers.[1] After that, an

---

[1] This was especially designed to allow villagers to arrange a compromise, thus making an electoral contest unnecessary. The prevailing sentiment in the Panchayat Raj Department in Tahsil Headquarters (as well as State Government policy), was that contested elections were to be discouraged since they

election was automatically scheduled for any post in which the number of candidates exceeded the number of seats available.

It is important to remember the existence of the deadlines for filing and withdrawal, for once each deadline passed, the village was bound by law to act in terms of the situation which was thus created. When the deadline for nominations was passed the villagers were limited in their choice to those men who were nominated for the post of pradhan. They were not allowed to add a new candidate for the office. Once the deadline for withdrawals was passed it was not possible to have a candidate's name stricken from the record. As we will see below, at one stage, after the withdrawal deadline, consideration was given to having all candidates for the post of pradhan withdraw their names. (It would seem that if the Panchayat Raj Department had been confronted with a situation of this nature it would have been forced to make an ad hoc arrangement for the postponement of elections.) The important fact is that the villagers did not become aware of these procedural limitations until they had been overtaken by them.

Let us resume the account of the pre-election, pre-nomination manoeuvering. In the week prior to the filing of nomination papers, the names of the individuals who had appeared at the Panchayat Raj Department office in Tahsil Headquarters to "purchase their tickets" became known. The date for filing nomination papers

---

tended to bring out into the open many disputes and quarrels of long standing. The effect of this, it was felt, would be to destroy the possibility of future harmonious cooperation. Such action need not have meant the retention of the old pradhan, though many villagers feared this would be the result if a compromise were arranged.

with the Returning Officer, i.e., the last day that a candidate could enter the race, was set for November 18. On the Sunday prior, November 13, an attempt was made by several rajpūts of B borough to call a general meeting panchayat to decide: (1) on a candidate who would be supported for the post of pradhan, and (2) on a list of candidates for the gaon and adalat panchayats. The belief of those supporting this move was that if the village could be made to agree on one set of candidates, then all others who may have purchased "tickets" would feel obliged to withdraw. In this way a contested election would be avoided. Many villagers seemed to feel that an electoral contest would be a bad thing, though the reasons for their belief differed. Almost all agreed that it would cause trouble in the village.

The panchayat called for the 13th of November was not held. Many important village leaders were absent; in some instances purposefully. Also, the Principal of the secondary school made known his opposition to a meeting at that time. He felt such a meeting would have to be properly timed in order to achieve the maximum benefit. His intention was to call a meeting a day or two prior to election day of all candidates who had not withdrawn. Any meeting attempting to bring about a compromise which was held earlier than that would, in his view, be premature.

While the power of the old pradhan had been declining, the Principal had bided his time and functioned as an intermediary between the villagers and "the outside world." His most effective connections were with the Congress Party apparatus and the staff of the Community Development Programme. An educated and articulate man, the Principal became an important figure in the politics of the Tahsil. The secondary school, which was a show place of the area in any event, became a stop on the itinerary of all important visitors to the District. His position in the village became progressively more important, and by the time of the second village elections it was clear that he envisaged a decisive role for himself in the proceedings.

Up to the time of the election the Principal had concerned himself with village affairs in such a fashion as to avoid direct involvement in factional quarrels, and was able to maintain a position of neutrality in which he carried on activities for the good of the entire village. When he began to involve himself in the politics of selecting a new pradhan, his impartial position was damaged. Many villagers strongly resented the intervention of "an outsider" in their affairs.

Despite the refusal of the Principal, noted above, to participate in a panchayat to solve the problem of who would become the new pradhan, the demand for such an informal panchayat grew stronger. Finally, two days later, on November 15, a general meeting panchayat was again called. Forty people attended, of whom 32 were rajpūts. The failure of most other castes to participate, and therefore be bound by the decisions of the panchayat, was critically noted by those attending. None of the men who were known to be candidates came in person, but it was soon evident that each was represented by an agent. After a prolonged discussion, it was decided that a committee to consist of one rajpūt from each of the seven boroughs, a brahman, a banyā, and an untouchable would be chosen and given the task of selecting an acceptable candidate for pradhan. Despite the agreement in in principle, a sharp discussion ensued as to who would actually represent each group. Gopal Singh, a rajpūt of *A* borough, who was the sarpanch of the adalat panchayat, succeeded in dominating the entire proceedings and pressed his own selections for the committee on the group. Considerable dissatisfaction was voiced by members of the panchayat as the selections were being made. It was evident that several of the men chosen were opposed by a substantial segment of those present.

As soon as the members of the committee stepped outside to deliberate, open criticism was levelled at Gopal Singh and at the method of carrying out the proceedings thus far—one member of the panchayat criticized the notion that ten people should decide a question which affected 5,000. (The fact that he had agreed upon this method of choice in the hopes of seeing his own men on the committee did not seem incongruous to him.) Another member of the panchayat pointed out that the rajpūts of *G* borough were not represented on the committee and therefore would not be bound by its decision. At this point several of the people began to leave the meeting hall and the meeting ended in failure.

The point which no one at that time brought forward was that this was the last opportunity to arrive at a decision and still be able to add the name of the compromise candidate to the slate of candidates. Henceforth they would be bound to choose from among the candidates who had filed nomination papers. The only possible exception, as noted above, was if all candidates who had filed for the post of pradhan turned in their nomination papers before the final withdrawal date. However, if one of them refused to do this the compromise could not be carried out.

The last day for the withdrawal of nomination papers was November 28. On November 27 an attempt was again made to bring about a compromise. Nomination papers for the post of pradhan had been filed by five rajputs, one each from *A*, *B*, *C*, *F* and *G* boroughs, as well as by a chamār from *F* borough. The candidacy of the rajputs from *A* and *C* boroughs was half-hearted. Further, most people felt that few, save the untouchables, would vote for the chamār candidate.

At the general meeting panchayat called for the 27th of November there were 63 persons present, of whom 45 were rajputs. The other castes were somewhat better represented than they previously had been. However, only one of the six candidates for the post of pradhan was present; the rajput from *F* borough. Only he, in theory, could be bound by the decision of the panchayat. In discussion with the supporters of two of the other rajput candidates it became evident to this writer that they were intent upon forcing an election, confident of their ability to succeed. As soon as the panchayat started these men began engaging in tactics designed to obstruct the holding of the meeting. Several groups of rajputs, when asked whom they would be willing to support as a compromise candidate, refused to commit themselves. They demanded more time for consideration of the matter and offered to give their views in a few days. This attitude, coupled with the absence of five of the six candidates for the post of pradhan, soon convinced all present that nothing in the way of a compromise would be achieved at this meeting. The members began to leave.

One interesting point had developed in the course of the meeting. A rajput from *B* borough commented that everyone was too concerned with the question of who would be pradhan. "Emphasis should be placed on choosing honest members of the gaon panchayat and then it will not be necessary to worry about the pradhan," he argued. No one present agreed with this view, and he was soon shouted down.

The day for the withdrawal of nominations came and passed with all candidates refusing to turn in their nomination papers. A third, and final, attempt to decide upon a compromise candidate was made on December 10. The meeting had the largest attendance of such meetings in several years—100 people, representing 14 castes and all boroughs. (The total membership of the 14 castes represented comprised approximately 80 per cent of the population of the village. All of the principal castes were represented.) Four of the six candidates for pradhan personally attended, and principal supporters of the other two candidates were also present.

Soon after the meeting got under way Gopal Singh, who was a supporter of one of the two absent candidates, voiced the opinion that an election would not be a bad thing. Further, since two of the candidates were not present, he felt it would seem that they were desirous of an election. Therefore, he suggested, an election should not be opposed. This idea was shouted down.

Gopal Singh then informed the panchayat that it would be against the law for them to attempt to nominate a candidate who had not purchased a ticket—thus they were bound to choose from among the six candidates. He noted that only if all six withdrew would it be possible to choose a new man. If five withdrew and one refused then that man would automatically be elected. All present agreed that this was not desirable. Several people then suggested that each of the four candidates present, plus the principal supporters of the other two (of whom Gopal Singh was one), leave the meeting and decide amongst themselves whom they would be willing to support! The complete impossibility of such a move succeeding did not seem to be understood.

After some protest the six retired to a separate spot and began their discussion. The two "supporters" maintained that they were not empowered to withdraw their candidate's name, and one of them, Gopal Singh, after announcing this, left the group and returned to his home. The other five returned to the main panchayat and announced their failure. From this point on the futility of it all became increasingly apparent.

Several villagers suggested that an attempt be made to organize a committee, similar to the one organized in the first panchayat, which could be given the responsibility of deciding upon a compromise candidate.

In this connection it is interesting to note an aspect of the psychological impact of the State and its political programmes upon the village. Between the time of the first panchayat, mentioned above, and the present panchayat the villagers had been told something of the method to be used in the event of an election. The village was to be divided into four wards. An election would be held in each ward for candidates to the general membership of the gaon panchayat and, in addition, votes would be taken for each of the candidates for pradhan. Whereas the votes for pradhan would be added together from each of the four wards, the votes for general membership would be by individual wards. In this way the ward was to be given a sense of political distinctness. Whereas in the first panchayat when the suggestion to organize a committee to decide on a common candidate was made, the basis for organization and selection of rajput members was the borough, now the villagers spoke in terms of wards. It was suggested that two rajpūts be chosen from each ward and additional representatives of other castes be selected as before on a village-wide basis. No one seemed to raise any objection to the fact that the ward now rather than the borough was being used as the basis for representation within the panchayat.

As soon as an attempt was made to name rajpūts from each of the wards, dispute arose. No matter who was named there were those who would oppose him and question his judgment and impartiality. The arguments became more vociferous and finally the meeting broke down completely. Those present expressed a considerable degree of bitterness and resentment at the entire proceedings, and particularly with the two candidates who had not been present.

After it seemed certain that an election would take place political development in the village moved on to a second phase; that of attempts to form alliances. Before discussing them it may be worthwhile to stop at this stage and take note of those aspects of election procedure which had a bearing on the ability of the villagers to form alliances. The village was divided into four wards. The pradhan was to be elected by the entire village, though voting was to take place separately in each ward. The candidates for general membership were to be voted on separately in each ward. In the North Ward, for example, nine names were presented for seven vacancies on the panchayat. Only the voters in the North Ward would vote for these seven seats.

A unique factor regarding the election was that each voter was to be allowed as many votes as there were candidates. That is, since there were six candidates for pradhan, a voter legally could vote for all six. In this event, however, he would be cancelling his vote since he would have favoured none. However, it was possible for two candidates to form an alliance and agree to ask their supporters to vote for both of them. In this way they would combine their votes and would enhance their ability to defeat a common enemy. Multiple voting was possible both for the post of pradhan and for general membership on the gaon panchayat.

The second important factor to note is that the voting was to be open, not secret, and to be taken by a show of hands. In this way it was quite possible for all to see who in each borough had supported which candidates. This fact was most oppressive to the untouchables. Soon after the election became inevitable the untouchable residential areas (*bastis*) were increasingly visited by supporters of each of the five rajpūt candidates, alternating promises with threats and seeking the support of the untouchable groups for their candidate. The same type of pressure was applied to the members of the artisan castes.[2]

On December 12, a meeting was held between the rajpūt leaders of *C, D, E, F* and *G* boroughs. Previously

[2] The voting strength of each ward, according to the panchayat officers, was relatively equal. The total number of eligible voters in the village was between 2,600 and 3,000. Exact figures were not available and we were not permitted to review the electoral rolls. However, most villagers, in discussing the election, noted that there were about 2,000 votes available from the caste Hindus and Muslims and 600 from the untouchables. One fact which concerned many rajpūts was that if the five rajput candidates divided the 2,000 votes along relatively equal lines amongst themselves, the untouchable candidate, who could be presumed to receive all 600 of his votes, would be in a position to capture the post of pradhan. The existence of that solid block of 600 votes was one of the reasons for the repeated attempts to form alliances between several of the rajpūt candidates.

there had been separate meetings between rajpūts of
C, *D* and *E* boroughs, and also between rajpūts of
F and *G* boroughs. This attempt to unite these five
boroughs against the candidates of *A* and *B* boroughs
conformed to traditional village pattern of alliances.
Difficulties, however, were immediately encountered.
The least popular rajpūt candidate came from *G* borough.
Most other rajpūts in *G* borough refused to support
him. His principal supporters came from rajpūts in
C, *D* and *E* boroughs. An attempt was made in this
panchayat to persuade the *F* and *G* borough rajpūts to
support the *G* borough rajpūt candidate. This was
of no avail. The rajpūt candidate from *F* borough was
strongly opposed to this. The rajpūt candidate from *C*
borough was not present, but his supporters indicated
that he was not particularly interested in withdrawing
in favour of the *G* borough rajpūt either. After the
meeting had proceeded for some length and it developed
that no compromise could be agreed upon, one rajpūt
arrived and announced to all present that the Principal
was trying to bring about a compromise. To achieve
this he was attempting to meet with all six of the
candidates in an effort to persuade them to withdraw.
It was suggested that the present meeting be postponed
until the effectiveness of the Principal's attempt was
determined.[3] Therefore, the meeting disbanded.

[3] In this attempt to form an alliance along the old traditional
lines immediate difficulties were encountered. They stemmed
from the fact that existing alliances between rajpūt joint farm
families, and domains which had been created by clusters of
these joint farm families, were structured in such a way that they
crossed borough lines. The *G* borough rajpūt candidate for
example found allies in *C*, *D* and *E* boroughs who were in
opposition to some of the other rajpūts of *F* and *G* boroughs.
It would seem that they did not consider the threat posed by the
strong candidacy of the *B* borough rajpūt candidate to be of

(Despite the turn of events, no further attempt was made at a compromise between these five boroughs.)

The Principal began his efforts to have all candidates withdraw on December 12, three days before the election. He called in each of the candidates and their principal supporters and attempted to persuade them to withdraw for the good of the village in order that open elections and the quarrels which would result therefrom would be avoided. He promised each candidate that in the event all candidates withdrew a fair and open panchayat would be held and a pradhan acceptable to all would be chosen. Many of the villagers tended to fear this manoeuvre, seeing in it an attempt by the Principal to reinstate the old pradhan. A good deal of hostility was expressed toward the Principal. Most people resented his interference, but were waiting to see whether he would be successful. In the two days which intervened, December 13 and 14, the Principal was able to get signed statements from four of the six candidates agreeing to withdraw from the election. The two who refused to withdraw were the most open and vociferous opponents of the old pradhan. One was the rajpūt from *B* borough; the other the rajpūt from *F* borough.

As it later developed, both these men were induced to run by a rajpūt from *G* borough who was openly antagonistic to the Principal. Both rajpūts still contesting had sworn their loyalty to this man (Rup Singh of *G* borough), who at the time of the second elections was the largest landholder in the village. He had suffered the loss of a considerable amount of land due to the actions of the previous panchayat and held the Principal and the old pradhan responsible for his

---

sufficient danger to their respective positions to cause them to join in an alliance against him.

losses. It further developed that the rajpūt candidate from *G* borough who was involved in a dispute with Rup Singh, was secretly supported by the Principal.

The Principal was able to induce one of the two remaining candidates, the rajpūt from *B* borough, the younger of the two men, to withdraw his candidacy under the agreement that the final choice for pradhan would be made from among the six who had already purchased tickets.[4]

Only one candidate was left in the race, the old rajpūt from *F* borough who still refused to withdraw. Finally the Principal mustered all his support, sending men to him during the entire night of the 13th of December and early morning of the 14th. When it finally developed that the condition under which the other rajpūt, from *B* borough, had resigned could not in fact be enforced, this man bitterly castigated the Principal and made it clear he would never withdraw. Since he refused the Principal lost his gambit, and was forced to return the resignations to all the other candidates. The election was inevitable.

The conduct of the elections in Khalapur was as follows. The village, as we have noted, had been divided into four wards. The North Ward included

[4] A point of interest about this candidate. He was the son of the second sarpanch and mukhiyā of the village, who held office in 1929. The older rajpūt had been a supporter of the lower caste group which opposed the rajpūt in the first election in 1949. In the present election, his son again sought the support of the lower castes, and soon after his candidacy was announced he began speaking of his "labour party" (sometimes using the English words, although in Hindi he would call it the mazdūr party). To complete the analogy, it should be noted that during a heated discussion a supporter of the "labour party" candidate referred to one opposing candidate's party, in a sarcastic tone, as "the Churchill party."

all of *A* borough; the West Ward included all of *G* and part of *F*; the South Ward included the remainder of *F* and all of *B* borough; and the East Ward included all of *C*, *D* and *E* boroughs. The elections for both the pradhan and the gaon panchayat were held in each ward; there was no general meeting for the election of the pradhan. Each ward was allocated a set number of seats on the basis of its population. In filing for the election a candidate for a position on the gaon panchayat filed as a candidate in one of the four wards. A fixed number of seats were reserved for members of the Scheduled Castes (untouchables). In addition, three additional general seats were made available so that there would be a surplus of three members who could be chosen to serve on the adalat panchayat. Some of the candidates clearly announced this as their intention. The distribution of seats and candidates is indicated in Tables IV and V.

TABLE IV
SEATS AVAILABLE

Ward	Unreserved	Reserved
North	6	1
West	4	0
South	6	2
East	7	2
TOTAL	23	5
Total number of available seats	28	

The Election of the Second Gaon Panchayat

Table V
NUMBER OF CANDIDATES*

Ward	Unreserved	Reserved
North	9	0
West	5	1
South	4	2
East	8	1
Total	26	4
Total number of candidates	30	

* Three of the members elected to the gaon panchayat were to be selected to serve on the adalat panchayat. Both reserved and unreserved candidates were eligible. In the past, one untouchable, a chamār, was chosen to serve on the adalat panchayat.

In three of the four wards elections for general membership on the gaon panchayat were scheduled to be held, since the number of candidates exceeded the seats available. In the South Ward alone elections for general membership were not scheduled since there were fewer candidates than there were seats available. When questioned as to why they had not put up sufficient candidates, some of the residents of this ward commented that most of the inhabitants were peaceful men who did not like to get involved in quarrels. While this was a very charitable rationalization, the more accurate answer was that they were not clear as to the number of seats available to them.

In each ward an area was designated as the polling place. One portion was set aside for the ladies; one for the men. As the voters came to the polls the election officials assigned to each of the wards tried to get them to sit down in lines facing the desk set up for the Returning Officers. Each candidate for the post of pradhan, under the terms of the Panchayat Act and its Rules, had appointed an agent whose job was to scrutinize the proceedings and protect the interests of his candidate. This took the form of challenging persons seated among the voters whom they felt were not legally entitled to vote, i.e., minors, persons not registered on the electoral rolls of that ward, etc. In addition, at the time of polling the agents accompanied the Returning Officer as he walked up and down the lines of voters checking that an accurate count was being made.

When the voters had assembled in each ward the Returning Officer read off the names of all the persons who were candidates for the post of general member of the gaon panchayat and also for the post of pradhan. In those wards in which the number of candidates for general membership exceeded the vacancies, the Returning Officer then proceeded to call for a vote on each man. The voting was done by simply raising hands or standing up at the time the name of a man favoured was called. As we have noted earlier, since there was no way of effectively checking double voting, everyone was allowed to vote for each of the names proposed. Thus in the North Ward, where there were at the outset nine candidates for the six general member seats, a villager could have cast nine votes; one for each of the candidates in turn. Nine votes would have been the same as no vote; however, as best as could be determined, this situation did not arise to any significant degree in any ward.

An interesting situation arose in connection with the

elections to general member of the gaon panchayat. As noted above, in three of the four wards elections were due to be held. While the elections were actually in progress influential members of the boroughs in question circulated among the voters seeking out the candidates, attempting to persuade certain of them to withdraw to avoid the necessity of election. There was strong and open social pressure on these candidates to withdraw and thus avoid an election. In each instance it was successful. The issue was not so much the merits of the individual candidates, as it was the holding of an election. While votes were actually tabulated for general membership in two of the four wards, this was done for only the number of candidates necessary to fill the vacant seats. In none of the four wards were elections held for a general member which resulted in the defeat of a candidate.

The election for pradhan, however, was contested in all four wards. Two events which affected this contest had taken place on the morning of election day. The *C* borough rajpūt had announced that he had withdrawn his candidacy. No open announcement was made as to whom he wished his supporters to vote for. However, after the election it seemed obvious that his decision had been in favour of the *G* borough rajpūt. Also, the *A* borough rajpūt announced that he was withdrawing his candidacy and asked his supporters to vote for the *B* borough rajpūt. At the time of the balloting the names of both the *A* and *C* borough rajpūts were called, since they had not officially cancelled their nomination, and the *A* borough rajpūt polled 136 votes; 134 in his own ward.

The night before the election and the morning of election day were marked by an intensity of electioneering that would have made the old time political bosses in the United States envious. Agents continued to circulate until late in the night. It became increasingly clear that the election would be decided by the votes in the East Ward (*C*, *D* and *E* boroughs), since the two strongest candidates each claimed this area. The *B* borough rajpūt felt the majority of its votes would go to him since his "labour party" was presumably strong in this ward. The *G* borough rajpūt also claimed the ward, but said little to support his claim. The results of the voting for the post of pradhan are given in Table VI. The winning candidate, the rajpūt from *G* borough, received the bulk of his support in the East Ward: 428 of 635 votes.

As pointed out in the note to Table VI, it seems reasonable to assume that 41 per cent of the total votes cast were multiple votes. In most cases large blocks of votes were cast for two candidates in each ward, with the favourite son (rajpūt) receiving the votes of virtually all those present (this was least true of *A* borough). If, for the West Ward, the 485 "favourite son" votes are subtracted from the total votes cast—711—we see that about 226, or 31 per cent, of the ballots represented second or third ballots. Over half of these multiple ballots (127) were cast by the untouchables in voting for their own candidate. Double voting was most pronounced in the South Ward, where at the last moment an understanding was arrived at between rajpūts and untouchables that each would give full support to the other's candidate. The slightly smaller total for the chamār candidate is accounted for because the rajpūt women refused to vote for a chamār, even though their husbands urged them to do so.

The ratio of female to male voters at the polls was relatively low—about one to four. While men of all castes came to the polls, many rajpūt men indicated

The Election of the Second Gaon Panchayat

TABLE VI*

Candidate	North Ward	South Ward	East Ward	West Ward	Total
A borough rajpūt	134	—	2	—	136
B borough rajpūt	146	433	1	—	580
C borough rajpūt	—	—	—	—	—
F borough rajpūt	58	31	11	485	583
F borough chamār	28	359	98	127	610
G borough rajpūt	85	23	428	99	635
Total by Ward	447	846	540	711	2544

* The sum of highest votes polled in each ward may be taken as a fairly accurate index of the total turnout at the polls. Thus, 146, 433, 428 and 485 gives us 1,492 voters out of an estimated electorate of 2,600, or a 57 per cent turnout. If the figure 1,492 is used as the total voting strength, then it may be assumed that of the total 2,544 votes cast, 1,052, or 41 per cent, represent multiple votes.

that they did not wish women from their households to participate in the elections. Of the women who did attend, it seemed that most, if not all, did not fully realize what was going on. They knew that they had come to vote for a certain candidate, for they had been instructed to do so by their men folk, but they did not understand what specific actions were required of them. Thus in some instances they failed to stand up when the Returning Officer called the name of the candidate they were to support. Since the men were not permitted to communicate with them (though at times some tried), they stayed silent rather than commit an error. In all wards the Returning Officers read off a set of voting procedures prior to the actual balloting, but due to the turmoil and confusion while voters were coming in and being seated, many of the men, as well as the women, failed to understand the proper procedures.

A noticeable contrast between the first and second panchayat elections was the part played by the lower caste groups, particularly those which had been instrumental in organizing the brahman boycott after the election of the brahman pradhan in the village election of 1949. In the present election, while they made attempts to achieve unity of action, they met with much less success than before.

This time, rather than standing off in opposition to the lower caste groups, all the rajpūt candidates had vigorously sought their support. This began even before nominations were filed, and continued down to election day. It had been clear from the outset that several rajpūts would definitely be in the contest. Thus any lower caste candidate would be directly opposing a rajpūt. Many castes, especially the banyā, were reluctant to do this. The candidacy of the chamār, however, must be viewed in another aspect. Of all groups in the village the chamārs and other untouchables were most susceptible to rajpūt pressure. If a chamār were running—but not too seriously—the untouchables could reply to the pressure by saying, "Of course we owe our first allegiance to our own candidate, but then we shall try to support your man." As one chamār leader put it, the chamār candidate was a means of relieving pressure on the caste group. However, when the balloting took place, the untouchables in each ward voted for their candidate and then for the rajpūt candidate from that ward—very, very few deviated from this. That they came so close to success was somewhat of a surprise to them.

The artisan castes were not anxious to support the chamār; both because he was an untouchable and also, in their view, because he had little chance of success. They were forced to make a choice between the various rajpūt candidates. As the election drew near the *B* borough rajpūt spoke increasingly of his "labour party" and it seemed that many members of the artisan castes were favourably disposed toward him. Most felt that were he to be elected pradhan he would not exercise a harsh or oppressive policy toward them.

In the North Ward the principal candidate to be given support was the *B* borough rajpūt. The vote given to the "local candidate"—the *A* borough rajpūt—was "in error" since he had withdrawn. The vote for the *G* borough rajpūt was due to the fact that his principal political agent in the village was from *A* borough—and he exerted considerable influence over the leaders of several joint farm families. An analysis of the other wards shows that where a third or fourth candidate received votes in a ward it came largely from a dissident rajpūt group of joint farm families, rather than artisan and/or untouchable castes opposing the rajpūt candidate from that ward. From the results of the balloting it would seem that the non-rajpūt castes were not anxious to go against the dominant rajpūt group within their residential area with whom they had traditional farmer-retainer or other forms of contractual labouring relationships. On the day prior to elections a panchayat of all lower castes was held in an attempt to decide on a single rajpūt candidate to support. The meeting ended in failure.

The selection and support of candidates reflected, as could be expected, a basic struggle for control of the village between several groups. One was headed by Gopal Singh, rajpūt of *A* borough, who was sarpanch of the adalat panchayat after the first elections in 1949, and had been sarpanch of the old panchayat in the village from 1939-41. (He was also a relative of Sucheet Singh, the first sarpanch and mukhiyā of the village in 1920.) Gopal deserves to be styled "a charismatic leader," and the influence he continues to exert over the village, even over his enemies in the village, cannot be overestimated. Well educated, persuasive and perceptive, Gopal would have made the ideal village leader, save for his ability to be persuaded of the merits of a case by the amount of country liquor its proponent could supply. While most villagers were reluctant to entrust him with further public office, many readily followed his advice in the selection of pradhan. Gopal's support of the *G* borough rajpūt was based on a *quid pro quo* arrangement, for he had little personal attachment for this man prior to the election campaign.

The second man behind the scenes was the large landholder from *G* borough, Rup Singh. He opposed the old pradhan and was most anxious to prevent his candidacy, or bring about his defeat in the event he did run. To achieve this he asked two men to run, the *B* and *F* borough rajpūts. While he supported both equally at the outset, when the *B* borough rajpūt agreed to the Principal's plan for preventing an election without consulting him, Rup Singh became angered and withdrew his support. It is not surprising therefore that the *B* borough rajpūt received not a single vote in the West Ward. Had the support given the *F* borough rajpūt been given also to the *B* borough rajpūt the outcome would have been entirely different. In retrospect, on the basis of voting strength, the position of Rup Singh and his supporters was the strongest in the village, but due to their pique at the *B* borough rajpūt for yielding to pressures they materially affected their chances for success.

The Principal was the third man behind the scenes. At first he was most interested in seeking the re-election of the old pradhan, whom he had little difficulty in controlling and influencing. When this proved impossible, he persuaded the *A* borough rajpūt candidate to contest, for even though this man had little chance of success, his presence in the contest at least gave the Principal some bargaining power. The Principal was not at all certain of the *G* borough rajpūt candidate's ability to win, and although he secretly supported him, he was unwilling to commit himself openly.

Other individuals and groups attempted to influence the election, though they were much less effective. The most important of these was the group of rajpūts who had continued to support the old pradhan. When it was certain their man could not win again the group split; some stayed aloof from the election activities while others, mainly rajpūts from *B* borough supported the *B* borough rajpūt candidate.

The motivation to support a candidate on the part of each of these groups was to insure that its own position would be protected and a reasonable degree of personal aspiration would be aided and abetted by the "new administration." It is therefore most interesting to note that almost immediately after the election a split took place between the pradhan-elect, the *G* borough rajpūt, and his principal political agent, Gopal Singh, over the continued distribution of gifts and favours. The fear of an independent attitude by a successful rajpūt candidate toward his supporters, expressed by some at the time of the first election, was borne out by subsequent events.

VI
Conclusion

ONE of the principal sources of anxiety of many well-wishers of village panchayats in India—and especially of the Panchayat Raj Department of the Uttar Pradesh Government—is that village elections create more problems than they solve. In Khalapur the immediate results of the election would seem to bear this out. If, however, the election and related events are placed in proper perspective a somewhat different interpretation seems possible.

In the period following the elections the immediate effect of past events would seem to have been divisive. This is particularly true if one reviews (*a*) the effects on shramdan, (*b*) the effect of the village panchayat election on the General Elections held in the village, and (*c*) the effect on village factions.

In Uttar Pradesh the last week in January is designated shramdan week. It is an annual event. During this week all villagers are expected to offer shramdan; that is, to volunteer to do manual labour for the completion of some project of mutual benefit to the entire village. In the previous year villagers from all boroughs had volunteered their services to do earthwork on a road that was being built from the village to the local Tahsil Headquarters. It had been relatively successful, and while subject to the usual criticisms that rajpūts "supervised" while all others did the actual work, it had nonetheless been an effort supported by all villagers and openly opposed by none.

Conclusion

Shramdan week followed two weeks after the village elections. It had intially been hoped that work on some common project could be undertaken. This did not come about. Instead, separate projects were undertaken. Interestingly enough the old pattern of village alliances could be seen in this also. Thus C, D and E boroughs, led by the rajpūts there, worked on improving a road leading to the sugar cane mill used principally by the rajpūts of these boroughs. The A borough rajpūts worked on building up earthwork between the small stream which flows by the village and the road leading into their borough. In F borough there were two projects—each led by the unsuccessful candidates for pradhan from that borough. The rajpūts worked on improving the drainage on a road connecting their borough and G borough. This was to have been joined by a similar effort proceeding from G borough, but no spirit for shramdan could be aroused there. The hardest effort was put in by the F borough chamārs, who were digging a drainage ditch to connect a stagnant pond adjacent to their quarters, to the drains which led to the stream flowing by the village. They had been promised bricks from the Community Development Project to line the drain if they completed the earthwork.

Each of these projects was to be of benefit to the village, though more directly to the group carrying it out. Each rajpūt group castigated the others for the failure to agree on a common project, and was suspicious of the other's intentions. Even the impending visit of the late Lady Mountbatten to the village during shramdan week was not sufficient to heal the open breach in confidence and create a climate of co-operation. With the exception of the chamār project, the accomplishments of shramdan week in 1956 compared unfavourably with those in the previous year.

Although the General Election for the State and Central legislatures was still almost a year away, the spirit of faction and open division, intensified by the village election, had an effect on them. Of the two men which Khalapur participated in electing, the Member of Parliament and the Member of the State Legislative Assembly, the latter was most seriously affected. The Member of the State Legislative Assembly held a position as one of the Deputy Ministers in the Uttar Pradesh Government and had substantial influence in the sphere of planning and development. Villagers in the surrounding area felt that through his intercession Khalapur had received a disproportionate share of the development funds allotted to this particular Community Development Block. They felt this was due to the almost unanimous support given him by Khalapur in the first General Election of 1951-52. Whether there actually was intercession, and whether it was selfishly motivated, are not matters of vital concern here. Of importance is the fact that this view was widely held by all villagers in the area, including those of Khalapur who looked upon the man as a benefactor.

The Assemblyman was a staunch Congressman and the village had been almost 100 per cent Congress. The pradhan-elect, the *G* borough rajpūt, while not the most important Congress organization man in the area, was clearly identified with the Congress Party. The Congress Party had entered into agreements with other parties in the State not to contest, on a party basis, in the village elections, and the formal Congress organization did not in any way support the *G* borough rajpūt in this election. Still it was hard for many villagers to separate the man and his party. This was made even more difficult by the fact that the Principal, whose enemies in the village had come to be the same as those of the pradhan-elect

Conclusion

by the time of the village election, was also a Congressman. The linkage was made by many villagers that to the pradhan-elect and the Principal meant also to oppose the Congress. While caution must be advised in weighing the effect of the village election on the State election, still it should be noted that when the opposing candidate for the post of Member of the State Legislative Assembly, an Independent, came to this village the F borough rajpūt candidate acted as the sponsor of the meetings held in connection with his visit.

There is another factor which must be considered in this matter. Immediately after the village election several of the defeated candidates, and their supporters, decided to appeal the election in an attempt to have the results invalidated and a new election held. This was a process which the U.P. Panchayat Raj Department was reluctant to allow. One of the first men of importance approached by this dissident group, apart from those connected with the appeal procedure set forth in the law, was the State Assemblyman. The dissident group of villagers received a polite reply to their pleas from him, but were given no other support. The refusal to intercede was interpreted by some as a tacit admission of approval and support of the pradhan-elect. Despite the fact that support of the pradhan-elect was disavowed by the Assemblyman in a letter to one of the defeated candidates, the belief persisted to his detriment.

In the Second General Election in 1957 the incumbent Assemblyman was defeated in his constituency by 16,000 votes. He got 41,104 as opposed to 57,185 for the Independent candidate. Of particular interest is the fact that Khalapur, while still supporting the old Assemblyman, decreased its support from a near 100 per cent in 1951-52 to less than 66 per cent in 1957. Certainly other factors entered into his defeat in the constituency as a whole, but it is equally true that many local leaders were at a loss to explain precisely why his support in Khalapur had declined so sharply. It would seem that it must be understood, at least in part, in relation to the panchayat election.

The impact of the elections on village factionalism displayed several interesting aspects. In most instances the old divisions and animosities that had existed for years were reinforced. In other instances changes, which can only be described as remarkable, occurred. In the course of the campaign there had been no more bitter critic of the old pradhan than the F borough rajpūt. His sole purpose in contesting the elections was to insure the defeat of the old pradhan and his supporters. Yet immediately after the election these two men closed ranks and joined in drafting a petition against the pradhan-elect, and began devising strategies to oppose him. True, this was not a deep-seated change. Still the fact that they met publicly and worked together in an effort which called for some mutual trust must be noted. Obviously the "threat" to their respective positions posed by the pradhan-elect had been of a greater magnitude than their previous disagreement. Similar shifts in alignment took place between several groups which had formerly been in opposition to each other. By no means were the long-standing factional quarrels completely overcome; however, in some instances they had been bridged. If these strong antipathies can be overcome by an essentially "negative" factor, one is led to wonder whether an appeal for unity, skillfully based on a "positive" factor, might not be equally effective. By "positive" factor I mean some appeal to action which would benefit both parties and the entire village as well.

While it is customary at this stage to enter a disclaimer

Conclusion

in respect of the ability to generalize about the working of panchayats from a particular case study, this writer feels that the study raises certain considerations which merit further attention. This is particularly true with respect to the problem of creating institutions of local self-government in the Indian villages, able to assume the enhanced and more difficult burdens envisaged for them in current development planning. The problems cannot be solved by styling villages "a sink of localism, a den of ignorance," and thus writing them off. A charge so extreme is simply not justified, regardless of the eminence of its author.[1] Implicit in many rejections of the panchayat is a mistaken notion of the functioning of local government in modern democratic states. In addition, this writer feels there have been errors in judgment in assigning certain functions to the panchayats *at the present stages of their development*.

In an agricultural economy, characterized by a scarcity of cultivable land, the right to own and/or cultivate land gains central importance. This condition of land scarcity has persisted throughout North India for a considerable period of time. One of its immediate consequences, as we have seen, has been to make access to, and ownership of, cultivable land a principal source of controversy and factionalism. No matter how fair and impartial a panchayat were to be, any decision it made regarding these matters would have inevitably embittered the unsuccessful parties and thus generated resentment toward it. It is not disputed that ideally the village panchayats should assume the various functions of land management, maintenance of land records, the right to authorize and enter land transfers, partitions, amalgamations and other mutation proceedings. The crucial

[1] Dr. B. R. Ambedkar, *Constituent Assembly Debates*, Vol. VII, No. 1, p. 39.

element is the timing of the transfer of this responsibility. The institution, as presently constituted, is in its infancy. The procedures and duties of the panchayat in Khalapur were unknown to even the members of that body. The position of the institution in the village had not been stabilized. Only after it has functioned for a considerable period of time can it be expected to merit the confidence of the villagers in the discharge of tasks which have long precipitated factional strife.

When the panchayat was simply associated with the land consolidation programme little controversy arose. When actual control over aspects of land tenure and ownership were turned over to it, under the Zamindari Abolition Programme, a different situation arose. To have proceeded in haste in this connection may well have resulted in damaging the ability of panchayats to merit confidence of villagers for a significant period of time to come.

In this connection it should be noted that numerous sources have suggested that panchayat functions be graded into several classes, ranging from the simplest and least controversial on up. Each panchayat would then be assigned a certain class of functions, depending upon the evaluation of the Panchayat Raj officials. Those villages which demonstrated an absence of factionalism would presumably be given the greatest powers. The difficulty here is that the main criteria suggested for determining the existence or absence of factionalism in a village is to see whether the village elections have been unanimous. The assumption is made that in the event of an unanimous election village leadership is cohesive and factionalism is absent. But will this be uniformly true? One need but reflect on the situation surrounding the first panchayat elections in Khalapur to realize the errors in judgment that this might lead to.²

Gradation of panchayat powers has much to commend it, both as a practical reaction to a difficult situation and also as a means of disciplinary action directed at malfunctioning bodies. The ability to associate prestige and status with the granting of "Class A" powers would make their withdrawal by the State Government and the down-grading of the institution to a "Class B" or "C" body a useful though extreme sanction. The reverse operation would provide a source of commendation and incentive that would cost the State absolutely nothing.

The importance of the village panchayat for village economic and social development is fundamental. This is particularly true for those projects which are non-controversial in nature. In the period following 1949 three major projects of an essentially non-controversial nature were instituted in Khalapur: the building of the panchayat ghar (village community hall); the building of the secondary school; and the paving of the village lanes. In the process of implementing these three projects the villagers cast serious doubt upon several current erroneous beliefs concerning village development work.

---

² A similar error, in this writer's view, is that made by Jayprakash Narayan and his supporters who oppose village elections on the ground that they create village factions. To say this is to mistake cause for effect. Elections in rural India offer an opportunity for competing groups within the villages to manifest their opposition. They reflect village factions and admittedly may even heighten tensions between them, but it is erroneous to say that elections cause factions. Factionalism existed in rural India long before statutory electoral procedures were introduced. It is interesting to compare, in this connection, the extent to which the court system, introduced by the British, another "modern" political innovation, has been used by competing factions in rural India as yet another context within which they could pursue their existing factional disputes.

First, a problem repeatedly stressed is that of arousing sufficient enthusiasm on the part of the villagers to participate in development work. In all three instances the villagers were convinced of the merits of the programme and a substantial amount of enthusiasm and cooperation was generated. Second, it is often held that while the villagers may desire a certain project, they are not able to support it financially. In all three instances after the project was agreed upon financial support was forthcoming. Granted in the case of the panchayat ghar a major portion of the funds came from land sales; however, the previous tax record demonstrates that there was an adequate taxation base in the village to support such a project. The principal difficulty lay in the actions of the pradhan and the resultant distrust and lack of support for his efforts. The adequacy of the tax base in the village for development work was demonstrated beyond a doubt in the case of the school and village lane construction projects. In both instances the land-owning rajpūts, convinced of the necessity of the projects agreed to pay a variety of ad hoc taxes (Rs. 30 per plough; Rs. 30 on their cane payments, etc.) in order to support these projects. Funds were forthcoming when the need and desirability of a project was adequately demonstrated and where trust could be placed in the body managing the funds.

Another problem concerns the officers of the various State programmes who come into contact with the villagers and the officials of the panchayats. The contrast between the effectiveness of the Assistant Consolidation Officer, as opposed to the Village Level Worker of the Community Development Programme, or the Panchayat Secretary of the Panchayat Raj Department was marked. While the differing content of the three programmes must be weighed in any comparative evaluation of these

Conclusion

three men, still the maturity and personal effectiveness of the Assistant Consolidation Officer played a decisive role in the differing reception accorded his programme.

Perhaps the most important consideration, however, relates to the comparative emphasis placed on material accomplishments and procedural niceties, as opposed to the development of self-reliance and effective ability to operate the institutions of local self-government. Here the main remedy is undoubtedly a greater contact between the officers of a programme and the villagers, with a continuing stress on educating the villagers to their responsibilities and potentialities and the development of competent local leadership. What is required is a fundamental change in social orientation away from a satisfaction with the status quo to one in which change is not only accepted but desired. If this is to be of a continuing effectiveness, the villagers must be brought around to the condition where the major initiation and assumption of responsibility springs from institutions which they control and which are operated by them. The greatest danger in rural development work lies in the lapse that it seems will inevitably occur after the intensive phase of the Community Development activity is passed and the area reverts to what is known as a normal block. In this phase budget and personnel allotments are diminished and it is assumed that the villagers will take on these responsibilities. Unless they have been awakened to them, and local leaders have been developed and trained, there will be a period of sad disappointment in which even the limited accomplishments of the past are allowed to fall away due to a failure to maintain them. This is even more urgent in those states now adopting the system of Panchayati Raj.[3]

---

[3] See R. H. Retzlaff, "Panchayati Raj in Rajasthan," *Indian Journal of Public Administration*, Vol. VI, No. 2, *passim*.

In the past, when the official hierarchy has desired the completion of a task, the inevitable process of numerous lower echelon officers converging on a village and stirring up an unenthusiastic citizenry to a limited amount of endeavour has taken place. In most cases all that is accomplished is that a few hundred yards of a road is paved or a few more bricks are laid on a new hospital. Continuing supervision with a view to drawing in local leaders and giving to them some of the responsibility just has not been carried out. At all levels the stress on "showing results" as opposed to creating a genuine enthusiasm and ability to accomplish them on the part of the villager has been decried. But the process continues.

In looking back on the events in Khalapur, a most heartening aspect was the changes that have occurred in the village outlook simply due to the experience of six years of local self-government. The newness and strangeness of the institutions cannot be underestimated. The idea of voting in local assembly; of some groups acting in a constructive fashion as a check on the majority; of levying taxes on themselves to support projects which they themselves wanted to initiate, all of this was new, strange and confusing to the villagers. When to this was added the attempt to give them control over a matter which has long been a subject of controversy and factionalism, land, the resulting difficulty and confusion can be appreciated.

A remark made by one of the leaders of the village is most pertinent here. I had just finished a lengthy interview in which many of the shortcomings of the first panchayat had been discussed. He concluded his remarks by saying: "Don't forget this. This is the first time we have had such a thing in Khalapur. We have made many mistakes, but we will not make them again.

Conclusion

Now we have learned what the powers of the pradhan and the panchayat are. We will watch the new pradhan carefully."

Appendix A

FUNCTIONS OF GAON PANCHAYATS

OBLIGATORY FUNCTIONS

Article 15. Duties and functions.—It shall be the duty of every gaon panchayat so far as its funds may allow to make reasonable provision within its jurisdiction for:

(a) construction, repair, maintenace, cleansing and lighting of public streets;

(b) medical relief;

(c) sanitation and taking curative and preventive measures to remove and to stop the spread of an epidemic;

(d) upkeep, protection and supervision of any building or other property which may belong to the gaon sabha or which may be transferred to it for management;

(e) registering births, deaths and marriages, and maintenance of the register mentioned in section 9;

(f) removal of encroachments on public streets, public places and property vested in the gaon sabha;

(g) regulating places for the disposal of dead bodies and carcasses]* and of other offensive matter;

(h) regulation of melas, markets and hats within its area, except those managed by the State Government [or the district board] and without prejudice to the provisions of the U.P. Melas Act, 1938;

(i) establishing and maintaining primary schools for boys and girls;

(j) establishment, management and care of common grazing grounds and land for the common benefit of the persons residing within its jurisdiction;

(k) construction, repair and maintenance of public wells, tanks and ponds for the supply of water for drinking, washing and bathing purposes, and regulation of sources of water supply for drinking purposes;

* Bracketed material added by amendments to original Act.

(*l*) regulating the construction of a new building or the extension or alteration of any existing building;

(*m*) assisting the development of agriculture, commerce and industry;

(*n*) rendering assistance in extinguishing fire and protecting life and property when fire occurs;

(*o*) the administration of civil and criminal justice;

(*p*) the maintenance of such records relating to cattle census, population census and other statistics as may be prescribed;

(*q*) maternity and child welfare;

(*r*) allotment of places for storing manure [and for tanning and curing of hides];

(*s*) fulfilling any other obligation imposed by [or under this Act or] any other law on a Gaon Sabha;

[(*t*) the maintenance and control of class (1) and Kaiser-i-Hind forests, waste land (benap), water channels and drinking places (panghat) in the hill patties of the Kumaon Division].

Discretionary Functions

Article 16. A gaon panchayat may also make provision within its jurisdiction for

(*a*) planting and maintaining trees at the sides of public streets and other public places;

(*b*) the improved breeding and medical treatment of cattle and prevention of disease in them [including the maintenance of pedigree bulls];

(*c*) filling in of sanitary depressions and levelling of land;

(*d*) organizing, subject to rules prescribed, a village volunteer force for watch and ward, for assisting gaon panchayat and [nyaya panchayat] in the discharge and notices issued by them;

(*e*) assisting and advising agriculturists in the obtaining and distribution among them of Government loans and in the repayment thereof, in the liquidation of old debt and generally in the establishment of sound credit system according to law;

(*f*) development of co-operation and establishment of improved seed and implement stores;

(*g*) relief against famine or other calamity;

(*h*) making representation to the district board for performance by it of such functions in relation to the area within the jurisdiction of the gaon sabha as is beyond the powers of the gaon sabha;

(*i*) extension of the abadi (and provision for house sites for weaker section of the public);

(*j*) establishment and maintenance of a library or reading room;

(*k*) establishment and maintenance of an akhara or club or other place for recreation and games;

(*l*) regulating the collection, removal and disposal of manure and sweepings [and making arrangements for the disposal of carcasses of animals];

(*m*) prohibiting or regulating the curing, tanning and dyeing of skins within 220 yards of the abadi;

(*n*) setting up organizations to promote goodwill and social harmony between different communities;

(*o*) public radio sets and gramophones;

(*p*) any other measure of public utility calculated to promote the moral and material well-being or convenience of the villagers;

(*q*) with the previous sanction of the district board the doing of anything which falls within the functions of the district board for the benefit of the persons living within the jurisdiction of the gaon sabha;

(*r*) the doing of anything the expenditure on which is declared by the State Government; or by the prescribed authority with the sanction of the State Government to be an appropriate charge on the fund of the gaon sabha; and

[(*s*) making arrangements for the seizure and disposal of stray cattle, stray dogs, wild animals and monkeys].

Appendix B

TAX SCHEDULE

Article 37. Imposition of taxes and fees.—(1) Subject to the rules made or directions given or restrictions imposed by the State Government a gaon sabha may levy

(*a*) in areas where the rights, title and interest of intermediaries have been acquired under section 4 of the Zamindari Abolition and Land Reform Act, 1950, a tax on land not exceeding one anna in a rupee on the amount of land revenue payable therefor:

Provided that where the land is in the actual cultivation of a person other than the person liable to pay land revenue therefor, the tax shall be payable by the person in actual cultivation;

(*b*) in areas other than those referred to in clause (a) a tax on rent not exceeding one anna in a rupee on the amount of rent payable by a tenant by whatever name called, under the law in force relating to land tenures:

Provided that where the land is in the actual cultivation of the person liable to pay land revenue therefor; the tax shall not exceed one anna in a rupee on the amount of land revenue for such land;

(*c*) a fee subject to a maximum of six rupees per annum on persons carrying on any trade, calling or profession within the jurisdiction of the gaon sabha:

Provided that in the case of theatre, cinema or similar entertainment temporarily stationed in the area of the gaon sabha, a fee not exceeding five rupees per diem may be levied;

(*d*) a tax payable by the owner thereof on animals and vehicles other than mechanically propelled vehicles kept within the area of the gaon sabha and plied for hire, at the rate

(*i*) in the case of animals, not exceeding three rupees per animal per annum;

(*ii*) in the case of vehicles, not exceeding six rupees per vehicle per annum;

Tax Schedule

(*e*) fees on persons, not being persons assessed to fee under clause (*c*), exposing goods for sale in markets, hats or melas belonging to or under the control of the gaon sabha concerned;

(*f*) fees on the registration of animals sold in any market or place belonging to or under the control of the gaon sabha;

(*g*) fees for the use of slaughter houses and encamping grounds;

(*h*) a water rate where water is supplied by the gaon sabha;

(*i*) a tax for cleaning private latrines and drains payable to the owners or occupiers of the houses to which the private latrine or drain is attached, where such cleaning is done through the agency of the gaon sabha; and

(*j*) a tax, not exceeding such rate as may be prescribed, on buildings owned by persons who do not pay any of the aforesaid taxes and whose annual income exceeds three hundred rupees.

[(2) The taxes, rates and fees under sub-section (1) shall be imposed, assessed and realized in such manner and at such times as may be prescribed.]*

---

* Bracketed material added by amendments to original Act.

Glossary of Terms and Names

ābādī	village residential area.
adalat panchayat	a judicial panchayat created under the U.P. Panchayat Raj Act of 1947.
āsāmī	a class of land tenants created under the U.P. Zamindari Abolition and Land Reforms Act, 1950.
badmash	a trouble maker, a bad character.
banyā	a caste group; traditional occupation: merchants.
bārhaī	a caste group; traditional occupation: carpenters.
bastī	a term used to describe the Scheduled Caste residential areas in the village.
bhangī	a Scheduled Caste group; traditional occupation: sweepers.
bhar̥bhuja	a caste group; traditional occupation: grain parchers.
bighā	a unit of land area measurement; 1 standard bigha equals 0.625 acres.
brahman	a caste group; traditional occupation: perform religious rites and ceremonies.
chamār	a Scheduled Caste group: have traditionally performed various occupations considered defiling, now largely landless agricultural labourers.
dhōbī	a caste group; traditional occupation: washermen.
gaon panchayat	an administrative panchayat created under the U.P. Panchayat Raj Act, 1947.
gaon sabha	the corporate body created for each gaon panchayat under the U.P. Panchayat Raj Act, 1947.
gaon samaj	the corporate body created for each village under the U.P. Zamindari Abolition and Land Reforms Act, 1950.

garariya	a caste group; traditional occupation: goat herders.
ghar	house or residence. Panchayat ghar can be translated as village community hall.
jajmān-parjan	term used to designate the traditional pattern of service relationships between land owning farmers and their retainers in Northern India. See also kisān-lāgdār.
jaṭiya chamār	a Scheduled Caste group; traditional occupation: leather workers and shoemakers.
kahār	a caste group; traditional occupation: water carriers.
kharīf	the autumn harvest season; also the crop which is harvested in autumn. See also rabī.
kisān-lāgdār	term used to designate the traditional pattern of service relationships in Khalapur. See also jajmān-parjan.
kumhār	a caste group; traditional occupation: weavers.
lambardār	a village official charged with the collection of land revenue for the government during the British period.
lohār	a caste group; traditional occupation: blacksmiths.
mahal	a term used to designate a unit of land area; a sub-division of a mazra.
mazra	a unit of land area for which separate land revenue records are maintained by the government.
mazdūr	labour, labourer.
mukhiyā	a village official who functioned as an agent of the police and who was charged with helping maintain law and order during the British period.
naukar	a servant.
naī	a caste group; traditional occupation: barbers.
nyaya panchayat	the new name of the judicial panchayat created under the U.P. Panchayat Raj Act, 1947.

Glossary of Terms and Names

panch	a judge, a member of a panchayat.
pradhān	the chief executive officer of the gaon panchayat.
rābī	the spring harvest season; also the crop which is reaped in the spring.
rajpūt	a caste group; the dominant landowning caste in Khalapur; traditional occupation: warriors or soldiers.
sarpanch	a chief judge, the head of a judicial panchayat.
shramdan	voluntary labour; literally a gift of one's own labour.
swāmī	a holy man.
tahsīl	an administrative unit; a subdivision of a District.
telī	a caste group; traditional occupation: oil pressers.
thākur	a term used to designate rajpūts.
thōk	a subdivision of a mazra; a unit of land area.

Index

Agrarian Prospect in India, The, 7n
Alexandrowicz, Charles Henry, 7n
Almond, G. A., 15n, 17n
Ambedkar, Dr B. R., 119n
American Anthropological Association, Annual Meeting, 59th., 14n
Andhra Pradesh, 9
Arya Samaj, 43
"Authority and Community in Village India," 16n

Baden-Powell, B. H., 27n
Bengal, 27n
Berreman, Gerald D., 14n
Biedelman, Thomas O., 14n
Braine, 48

Caste and Economy in the Himalayan Hills, 14n, 15n
Caste conflict, effects over panchayat raj, 53-61
Churchill Party, 103n
Coleman, J. S., 15n, 17n
Committee on plan projects *see* India, Planning Commission
Community Development Block, 116; and District levels, 9; programme, importance of, 122-3, *irt* Panchayat election, 88, 93; project, 5, 8, 115
Comparative Analysis of the Jajmani System, 14n
Congress Party, role...in Panchayat election, 45, 93, 116-17; District Congress policy, 89

Dandekar, V. M., 17n
Darling, 48
Decentralization of political power, 2
Democratic procedure, Western notion, 23-4
Deoband, district, 13
Dhillon, Harwant Singh, 32n
"Dominant Caste in Rampura," 14n
Dominant Caste Politics in a North Indian Village, 19n
Drinking of liquors, abolition of, 62-3

Economic and Social Effects of Jagirdari Abolition and Land Reforms in Hyderabad, 7n
Economic Function of Hindu Caste: The Jajmani System, 15n
Election dispute, 108-112
Evans-Pritchard, E. E., 32n

Fortes, M., 32n

Foundations of Local Self-Government in India, Pakistan and Burma, The, 16n

GANDHI, 1
Gaon Panchayat, functions: discretionary, 128-9; obligatory, 127-8; income of, 71-6
Gaon Sabha budget, 68-71
Glossary of terms and names, 133-5
Gopal Singh, 45, 94, 97-8, 111-13
Gould, Herald A., 14n
Group Dynamics in a North Indian Village, 32n
Gumperz, John J., 32n, 52n

HARPER, EDWARD B., 14n
Harrison, Selig S., 19n
Hindu jajmani system, 14n
"Hindu Jajmani System: A Case Study of Economic Particularism," 14n
"Hindu Jajmani System: The Paternalistic *vs.* the Exploitative Model," 15n
Hitchock, J. T., 19n, 32n, 33-4
Husain, S.M., 49n
Hyderabad, abolition of jagirdari and land reforms, 7n

INDIA, PLANNING Commission, 5-7; Committee on Plan Projects, report, 8n; Programme Evaluation Organization, 8n; Report of the Committee of the panel on land reforms, 7n
India, The Most Dangerous Decades, 19n
Indian Penal Code, 38

Jajman-parjan system, 14
Jayaprakash Narayan, 23, 121n

KHUDANPUR, G.J., 7n
Khusro, A.M., 7n

LAMBARDAR ROLE OF, 28-33, 37, 40-1
Land Consolidation Committee, functions of, 54
Land Management Committee, purpose of, 53-4, 77-80, 84
Land Revenue Department, 82-3
Land System of British India, 27n
"Language Problems in the Rural Development of North India, 52n
Leadership and Groups in a South Indian Village, 32n
Lewis, Oscar, 32
Lloyd, I., 19n

MAHALWARI SYSTEM, 27n, 28n
Mahar, Pauline M., 15n
Malaviya, H. D., 16n
Meerut Division, 27
Mehta Committee Report, 8

Montagu-Chelmsford reforms, 37
Mountbatten, Lady, visit to a village, 115
Mukhiya, role of, 37-40, 43

NATIONAL DEVELOPMENT COUNCIL, 8
National Extension Service, 5, 8
"Note on Sanskritization and Westernization", 20n
Nuer, The, 32n

OUDH CODE, 27-8

PANCHAYAT, function of first gaon panchayat, 62-89; functions: discretionary, 128-9, obligatory, 127-8
Panchayat administration, tax schedule, 130-1
Panchayat Raj, Act of 1920, 55, 90-1, 106; administration, 78-81; composition, 13-18, 50-2, department, 5, 70-6, 86-8, 91-2, 114, 117, 122-3; election of members, 54-61; election of Second Gaon, 90-113; election procedure, 91-101; General Election, effect of, 116-18; essence of, 6, 14-23, 121-2; introduction to, 49-61; membership, 15-21; power of, 1, 38-40, 52-4, its gradation, 121; role of 9-10, 51-5; sub-committees, 60; taxation problem, 73-87
"Panchayat Raj in Rajasthan," 123n
Panchayat Sabha budget, 68-73
Panel of land reforms reports, 7
Patwari, role of, 54
Planning Commission, *see* India, Planning Commission
"Political Role of India's Caste Associations," 19n
Politics of the Developing Areas, The 15n
Programme Evaluation Organization, 9, 32n; *see also* India, Planning Commission
Prohibition of liquor, 63

RAJASTHAN, 9
Rajeshwar Prasad, 17n
Rampur, village, 32
Reports of the Committee of the Panel on Land Reforms, 7n
Report of the Team for the Study of Community Projects and National Extension Service, 8n
Report of the U.P. Panchayat Raj Amendment Act Committee 53n
Reserve Bank of India, rural credit survey, 86
Retzlaff, R. H., 123n
Rowe, William L., 15n
Rudolph, Susanne H., 19n
Rup Singh, *irt*, election, 103, 112
Rural credit survey, 86
Ryotwari system, 27n

SAHARANPUR, DISTRICT, 13, 17n, 27
Saurashtra, 3
Sarpanch, Chief judge, functions, 38-43, 45-7
Shramdan, 40, 114-15
Srinivas, M. N., 14n, 20n
"Structure of Unilineal Descent Groups," 32n
Study of Panchayats, 8n
Sucheet Singh, 39-44, 89, 112
"Systems of Economic Exchange in Village India, 14n

TARLOK SINGH, 6, 9
Thorner, Daniel, 6-7, 9-10
Tinker, Hugh, 16n, 39, 46

UNITED PROVINCE, Panchayat Raj Act of 1920, 49, 51-2, 54, 57, 60n; of 1947, 49, 50; Act No. IV of 1920, 37n
United Province Land Revenue Act of 1901, 36
United Province Legislature, 37
Uttar Pradesh, Consolidation of Holdings Act of 1939, 82; of 1953, 52-3, 82, 84-5
Uttar Pradesh Panchayat Raj Act, 3-5

Uttar Pradesh Zamindari Abolition and Land Reforms Act of 1950, 52-3, 75n, 76-7, 80-1, 84

VILLAGE GOVERNMENT IN BRITISH RULE, 27-48
Village level worker, role, 88, 122
Village Organization, 13-26; changes in, 124
Village panchayats, creation, 2
"Village Panchayat and the Pattern of Village Development," 6n
"Village Panchayat as a Vehicle of Change," 7n
Village Panchayats in India, 16n

WISER, WILLIAM H., 14n
Working of Bombay Tenancy Act 1958, report of investigation, 7n

ZAMINDARI ABOLITION ACT, 6in
Zamindari abolition programme, 120
Zamindari system, 27n

Augsburg College
George Sverdrup Library
Minneapolis, Minnesota 55404